AF612564

Issues in TESOL

Issues in TESOL

Capstone Projects

David Kent

Copyright © 2021.
All rights reserved.

No part of this publication may be reproduced, distributed, or transmitted in any form or by any means, including photocopying, recording, or other electronic or mechanical methods, without prior written permission, except in the case of brief quotations embodied in critical reviews and certain other noncommercial uses permitted by copyright law.

Distributable Content: The author, and the publisher, grant permission for the copy and distribution of handouts and photocopiable material from this book for any and all instructional purposes.

Although every precaution has been taken to verify the accuracy of the information contained herein, the editor and publisher assume no responsibility for any errors or omissions. No liability is assumed for damages that may result from the use of information contained within.

ISBN: 979-11-6110-114-9

Woosong University Press.
Daejeon, Republic of Korea.

First Edition.

DEDICATION

For the students and alumni of the
TESOL-MALL graduate program at Woosong University.

CONTENTS

LIST OF FIGURES

ACKNOWLEDGMENTS

I wish to extend my deepest appreciation to my wife *Hyunhee* who has been very patient and understanding throughout the entire process involved with the production of this book. I would also like to thank *Noel David* for his suggestions regarding this text and for his patience.

PREFACE

Serving as a general introduction to the field, the *Issues in TESOL* book series aims to deliver insight into the many varied concepts and practices involved in the teaching of English as a second language (TESOL). Each book focuses on particular issues of TESOL that may prove to be important both over the various stages of a career as well as those that may be important to particular individuals. Of significance, the book series emerges to fill the needs of those who come to the education field from other disciplines; for those who may find themselves teaching without experience; for those interested in beginning a career in teaching English; for those in-service teachers looking to reground; and for those who are about to embark on TESOL certification. The intent is to provide an overview of the field for both native and non-native speakers of English that will help readers make connections between the various theoretical discourses, research, and teaching practices that are involved in the teaching of the language to others.

The series consists of five books:

Perspectives and Practice centers on aspects of second language acquisition and the place of educational theories in teaching. It reviews the frameworks behind the methods, approaches, and techniques applied to the teaching and learning of languages over time, particularly those that provide us with an understanding of how best to teach today. A variety of classroom management theories are discussed, with educational leadership, as well as the ethics, laws, rights, and responsibilities in teaching explored, with those influences affecting second language acquisition from language, planning and policy, to culture, identity, and intercultural communication also touched upon.

Implementations focuses on those practical aspects of concern to teachers such as how to frame lessons to engage students, the basics of applying classroom management, the delivery of appropriate teaching content, and the development of effective lesson plans.

Sound, Meaning, and Form covers those concepts that are of most importance for teaching the 'what' of language (pronunciation, vocabulary, grammar) as opposed to the 'how' (listening, speaking, reading, writing). The focus is on developing a means of understanding as to how best teach these aspects, along with how to best provide learners with the means of improving them. Relevant to this are key teaching strategies and techniques, along with efficient and effective assessment of learner knowledge and linguistic production.

Capstone Projects highlights the expectations and steps required to complete some of the final projects that are often linked to TESOL certification, from the practicum through to the portfolio and thesis. This will help any instructor if they wish to engage in further education at the graduate level as well as those who may have colleagues or family members beginning academic studies to become in education.

Resources, serves as an easy reference guide for the series. It contains all of the practical content in one volume, bringing together the photocopiable content and quizzes (with answer keys), a collated list of worthwhile websites and beneficial applications, and an extensive glossary of terms.

Organization of the Text

The word *capstone* comes from architecture and refers to the final decorative coping (i.e., capstone) that is laid at the completion of construction. In a way then, the capstone project undertaken in an educational setting is the final 'stone' that is laid as part of your academic experience. Such a project comes to symbolize the completion of your degree, serves to demonstrate your competency, and represents the peak of your academic accomplishments. As a project, it provides a means for faculty, peers, and future employers to easily recognize your level of competency.

Although the nature of capstone projects varies from university to university, in the educational field they typically involve:

1. *Practicums:* engaging in real-life problem-solving.
2. *Portfolios:* a reflection on lived experience.
3. *Theses/Dissertations:* original research.

This book examines the final projects that educators may need to complete if they intend to undertake accredited graduate level studies in the field of TESOL. It is intended to be read as a whole or in part by teachers, students, parents, and any other stakeholders who may be interested in the topics. Each part follows a similar layout, beginning with a short overview in order to situate the topics presented, followed by the main learning outcomes achieved by reading that section of the text. After presenting the content matter, each part then closes with suggested readings and a content review quiz (with an answer key) in order to help readers in solidifying learning outcomes. A range of photocopiable content that teachers can put to use with their classes is also provided for each section. A comprehensive glossary then provides definitions for the major terms and concepts presented by the text. Also included are some useful resources that teachers can turn to in order to help with instruction, to develop content, for planning and managing classes, and for engaging in professional development. The three major parts of the book are *practicum, portfolio,* and *thesis*.

In chapter one, *practicums* are covered. A practicum experience involves a combination of class observation, providing classroom assistance, and teaching classes. It typically serves as the capstone project to a certificate or diploma in TESOL. During the initial stages of a practicum, prospective and in-service teachers simply watch classes, record their observations, and ask questions of their supervisory teachers outside of class time. The practicing teacher will then be provided with guided assistance by their supervisory teacher, and then move on to ultimately teach a series of classes that involve supervisory teacher observation. This part of the book provides one means to achieve this process, and along with an accompanying series of templates in the appendices, it aims to help guide the practicing teacher through the completion of a practicum process. The goal behind completion of the practicum presented in this book is to help pre-service and existing teachers partner with others who can provide mentorship by directing their activities and giving them appropriate feedback on the work that they may perform. The objectives of this section include: providing readers with a means of being able to critically analyze and evaluate the delivery of learning, demonstrate effectiveness in developing student competence through TESOL, showing that they can incorporate materials and resources into lessons to create a dynamic teaching environment appropriate to the language level and cultural context for language learners, and to show how they are able to engage in life-long learning by seeking out and undertaking their own professional development.

In chapter two, *portfolios* are covered. The portfolio typically serves as a capstone project to courses such as a master's in TESOL, and it is typically undertaken by those students who do not wish to complete a thesis. It serves as a means for prospective and in-service teachers to showcase their learning and the coursework that they have competed while undertaking graduate study, consider their competency as a classroom teacher, and engage in the reflection of their learning. The chapter focuses on the importance of a portfolio, and the place of reflection in its development. Also considered are the place of the advisor and the time requirements for portfolio submission. The very basics of what is involved in developing a portfolio is provided, with particular emphasis on the kind of work products that might be included, as well as the need to contextualize the teaching philosophy and goals, teaching methods and strategies, activities undertaken to improve teaching, and future goals within those reflections. An example portfolio, with the means used to evaluate and submit it to one particular graduate program, is also presented.

In chapter three, *theses* are covered. The thesis track in a master's graduate program typically consists of four basic components: successful completion of coursework, the candidacy examination, the formation of a thesis committee, and the writing and oral defense of a thesis project that follows a specific timeline. This track is typically undertaken by those students who intend to go on to doctoral level studies. The completion of a degree thesis as the capstone project serves as a means for prospective and in-service teachers to conduct an original study and perform critical analysis on a topic of their own interest. The chapter covers the rationale behind the writing of a thesis, and the need to follow a strict completion timeline. The role of advisors and students in the development of a thesis are also presented, as is the critical need to consider ethical implications when undertaking research. Scholarly rigor and academic misconduct are briefly discussed, as is what constitutes a thesis proposal. The typical sequential style thesis layout is then introduced along with the stages of a typical oral defense, and the means of finalizing the thesis project.

It is hoped that this book will provide both education and something new for all teachers – be they trained or untrained, pre-service, in-service, or retired.

David Kent.

PRACTICUM

1. The Practicum Experience

Overview

The practicum typically serves as a capstone project to courses such as a certificate or diploma in the teaching of English to speakers of other languages (TESOL). It serves as a means for prospective and in-service teachers to showcase their learning, exhibit competency as a classroom teacher, participate in professional dialogues with cooperating teachers, and engage in professional development to assist in life-long learning and ongoing teacher development. Ultimately, the practicum component assists prospective and in-service teachers in identifying their limitations while exploring and developing the skills to overcome these during the perfection of their craft.

Learning Outcomes

1. Understand what constitutes a practicum, and critically analyze and evaluate the delivery of learning.
2. Know the role of the academic advisor and supervisory teacher in practicum work, while demonstrating effectiveness in developing students' competence through TESOL.
3. Incorporate materials and resources in order to create a dynamic teaching environment, and design appropriate language lessons in accord with learning and cultural contexts.
4. Be able to show progress toward the development of a personal learning network through engagement in professional development activities.

The Practicum

The goal behind completion of the practicum presented in this chapter is to help pre-service and existing teachers to partner with others who can provide mentorship by directing their activities and giving them appropriate feedback on any work that they may perform. This chapter provides one means to achieve this process, and along with an accompanying series of templates, it aims to help guide prospective and in-service teachers through completion of the practicum process. If you are working, then you would be able to use the associated chapter templates to engage in a practicum aiming to develop your current teaching skills. If you are not currently working, then the same templates could be used if you were to volunteer with an organization offering free English language teaching services (such as a religious organizations), assisting you to develop confidence and competency while working alongside a teacher in a guided capacity.

A practicum experience involves a combination of class observation, providing classroom assistance, and teaching classes. During the initial stages of a practicum, prospective and in-service teachers simply watch classes, record their observations, and ask questions of their supervisory teachers outside of class time. The practicing teacher will then be provided with guided assistance by their supervisory teacher, and move on to ultimately teach a series of classes that involve supervisory teacher observation. If your practicum is part of a university degree, then it may also contain a link back to the relevant theory that you have covered in courses, and might involve the development of a pedagogy project in addition to the observational experience. Such programs also have students demonstrate how they will continue to engage in professional development once they leave such a program, and these components are also covered by this chapter.

VVAdvisors

Academic Advisor

A faculty member will serve as your advisor, and will be available to help guide you in the completion of your practicum by answering any questions that you may have about the process. They will help you to understand the tasks that you need to complete, and when the practicum is due. It is also the responsibility of the advisor to perform a final check of your submission, ensuring that everything has been completed satisfactorily. Once the completed practicum has been approved by your advisor, it will then be evaluated. In the case of a practicum, the submission is typically pass/fail but it may also be a graded pass. This evaluation would then accompany the bound submission of the practicum that you would need to provide to the graduate department office.

Supervisory Teacher

The supervisory teacher is the one that you will observe, the one who will observe you, and the one who will also comment on your practice and development as a teacher. They will prove invaluable to you as you can see how another teacher approaches the art of teaching and because they will also provide you with guidance and feedback on your own teaching. As each practicum can vary, this teacher may be a colleague that you trust and have asked to perform the duty, someone assigned by the principal of a school, or someone that you may have had to organize yourself by offering to volunteer with an organization or getting permission from an organization to deliver practice teaching in exchange for observing their teachers. Each particular organization will have its own privacy and confidentiality guidelines that you may need to follow.

Practicum Project Completion

There is a range of forms that need to be completed as you work through a practicum, and they a serve as proof of practicum completion. Once complete, they can be collated into a practicum portfolio, or become the basis of a teaching portfolio which instructors can then use to highlight their instructional abilities.

Requirements

Observation time requirements may vary from one academic institution to another, and from one degree program to another. For the examples provided in this text, the specified time of observation is a minimum of 15 hours (see Task 1) and this is split into 5 hours of self-observation, 5 hours of peer observation, and 5 hours of observation by a peer. How these hours are split is often negotiated with the supervisory teacher who you have chosen to help guide you through the completion of the practicum components. To help keep you on track, and to show how you have fulfilled these requirements, a timesheet such as that found in part A of the photocopiable section of this chapter would need to be completed.

Tasks

The tasks to complete for the practicum outlined in this text are:

1. Self-observation, and critical reflection
2. Peer observation, and evaluation
3. Clinical supervision (observation by a peer)
4. Pedagogy project (lesson plan development)
5. Engagement in professional development

Task 1. Self-Reflection – Logging to Learn

In environments where videotaping lessons is not appropriate (due to privacy or other ethical concerns), paper or electronic logs and checklists, as a form of teaching diary and feedback, can prove useful for gathering information and for being reflective in regards to your teaching. They can all allow you to keep track of what you do in your class, and how you do it.

In addition to completing the practicum observation hours timesheet for this task, you will need to keep a series of logs of how you perform as a teacher for at least five hours of class time and complete the appropriate section of the practicum template for this task (see the photocopiable section of this chapter).

1.1 You may decide to keep electronic or paper-based notes for your log, but you must complete the teaching log sheets with your practicum submission. So ensure that, however you keep your log, it can easily be transferred to these documents.

1.2 Select any lesson during which you teach normal classes (i.e., not an exam week, and probably not during the first few or last few weeks of the term or semester).

1.3 Select only one class that you teach, and focus on this class for the purpose of monitoring your teaching for this task.

1.4 Set aside a particular time of day when you can spend fifteen minutes completing your log. The best time might be directly after the class, or at the end of that work day. It is important to keep the log before you forget what has happened in the class. You may find it useful to take notes during the class, and refer back to these when preparing the log itself.

1.5 Try to be as specific as possible in your responses.

1.6 After completing the logs, distribute the student appraisal form to the same class (if the class is very large you can limit this to at least 5 students), and complete the self-evaluation checklist.

1.7 Take a close and critical look at all of your log entries, in light of the responses to the student appraisal form and the self-evaluation checklist, in order to get a clear and coherent picture of your teaching acts during the period of task one completion.

1.8 Engage in self-reflection, and complete the self-reflection questions form.

1.9 All forms required for completion of this task are found in the photocopiable content section of this chapter under part A (timesheet) and part B (task one).

Task 2. Peer Observation and Evaluation

Peer observation provides both the observer and the observee with the opportunity to mutually enhance the quality of their teaching practice. It also provides teachers with a chance to share good practice methods, approaches, and techniques, while also sharing their thoughts on the practice of teaching and supporting each other in the development of their instructional skills. As with task 1, for this task, you will need to complete the appropriate practicum sections of the observation hours timesheet, and the practicum template.

2.1 Find a teacher, or teachers, who will allow you to observe a total of five hours of their class time.

2.2 You will need to inform each teacher of the things that you will be doing while you are observing them, and share with them your observations post-lesson.

2.3 You will need to complete a series of nine worksheets during this observation period. The first five worksheets can be completed across a single lesson if desired, and will likely take an hour and a half of observation time. The remaining four worksheets can be completed over one hour of observation time each.

2.4 All forms required for completion of this task are found in the photocopiable content section of this chapter under part A (timesheet) and C (task two).

2.5 In addition, information on the observation process has been included in the photocopiable content section of this chapter under part D. It would prove worthwhile to have all of the teachers that you observe, and those who intend to observe you, read over this information.

Task 3. Clinical Supervision – Observation by a Peer

Clinical supervision is a process by which a teacher receives individualized support to enhance their instruction in order to improve education for their learners. It is often used as a term to mean the coaching of novice teachers. In this process experienced teachers are relied upon as trusted colleagues rather than as evaluators.

3.1 Find a teacher, or teachers, who are willing to observe five hours of your class time and complete the appropriate sections of the practicum template.

3.2 Each teacher that observes you will need to complete an a) pre-observation feedback form and a b) peer observation form for each lesson that they observe.

3.3 You will need to complete the pre-observation feedback form in advance so that the teacher who is observing you can make appropriate comments on it.

3.4 The clinical observation form can be completed by the teacher observing you as they sit in upon your lesson.

3.5 You should aim to discuss the comments on both forms with the teacher that is observing you, and this should occur in a pre-lesson observation briefing and in a post-lesson discussion. These discussions do not have to be lengthy but they give you the opportunity to understand the comments and to ask questions of the teacher observing you, as you go through the process of observation.

3.6 All forms required for completion of this task are found in the photocopiable content section of this chapter under part E.

Task 4. Pedagogy Project – Lesson Plan Development

Learning to plan and evaluate an effective lesson is an essential skill of being a teacher. This task will engage you in the development of a lesson of your choosing. However, you will need to demonstrate how you can adapt the concepts touched upon during your TESOL coursework to your specific teaching/learning context. You will then need to teach this lesson, and perform an appropriate evaluation and assessment of the lesson and your teaching effectiveness prior to completing the appropriate sections of the practicum template.

4.1 Use the provided templates to help you complete this project.

4.2 Develop a comprehensive lesson plan, modifying the templates as required to suit your teaching context and learner needs.

4.3 Link the implementation of the lesson plan to theory.

4.4 Reflect on the implementation of the lesson, and provide an evaluation of the created content and its use as part of a pedagogy project report.

4.5 All forms required for completion of this task are found in the photocopiable section of this chapter under part F.

Task 5. Professional Development – Lifelong Learning

The challenge for many practicing teachers, especially those in the English as a foreign language (EFL) teaching context, is a lack of exposure to professional development during their career. A means of obtaining professional development, and ways to interact with fellow teachers are to join local language teaching organizations or groups, to attend or present at their conferences, and to engage with group members in online forums or special interest groups. All of this will form part of your personal learning environment; in other words, the way that you organize professional development and the system that you put in place to manage your own learning over time.

5.1 For this task you will need to show progress toward the development of a personal learning network (PLN) through engagement in professional development activities, or through participation or involvement in a local teaching organization or group (either online or in person), documenting this in the appropriate section of the practicum template.

5.2 Choose an organization that you will begin to interact with. In the Republic of Korea for example, there are KOTESOL (Korean Organization for Teaching English to Speakers of Other Languages), KATE (Korean Association for Teaching English), and STEM (Society for Teaching English through Media) to name a few.

5.3 Decide which component of this task you will complete: conference attendance, conference presentation, or online participation. Conference attendance is advised, and many universities put these on for free to the public after registration. Sydney University in Australia hosts their annual TESOL colloquium for such purposes. Other institutions and professional organizations may host conference presentations online, and you may choose to view one, or some, of these.

5.4 All forms required for completion of this task are found in the photocopiable section of this chapter under part G.

Undertake **one** of **5.5**, **5.6**, or **5.7**.

5.5 Conference Attendance Steps

- **a.** Attend a conference, physically or virtually, and take notes from the presentations that you attend. You should attend at least three presentations.
- **b.** Prepare a summary of each of the presentations with an associated learning comment that details something new that you learned from the presentation, points that you found interesting, and something that you found that you could apply with your learners or adapt to your teaching context (current or potential). The summary should be in point form with the learning comment in either point or paragraph form.
- **c.** Use the forms in part G1 to help you complete this task, and submit the certificate of conference attendance (if you have been provided one).

5.6 Conference Presentation Steps

- **a.** Prepare an abstract to submit to one of the local organizations for potential presentation. You will need to review the specific calls for papers on their websites for the details regarding this.
- **b.** Once your abstract has been approved for presentation, prepare the paper and PowerPoint according to the organization's guidelines.
- **c.** Present the paper, and include both a copy of it and the certificate of presentation within your practicum portfolio as proof of completing this task.

5.7 Online Forum Participation Steps

- **a.** If you are unable to attend or present at a conference then the online forum participation option is available to you.
- **b.** Join an organization forum, a special interest group (SIG), or Facebook group.
- **c.** Post a number of questions related to your current teaching context, and answer the responses from group members. Questions might include aspects of classroom management, dealing with disruptive students, and managing teacher-talk time. These will depend on individual teachers, and will likely stem from identified shortcomings or other aspects related to the observation tasks. You will need to post a minimum of ten questions, add the screenshots of the post and any associated responses to your practicum template.
- **d.** You can use posts made to the learner management system during completion of your coursework for this component of the practicum, as that is considered a community of practice/organization forum.

Evaluation

The practicum component of a course is often evaluated by the head professor of a degree program or a designated faculty member who is known as your advisor. Often, practicums are graded simply as pass/fail but, as in the case for the practicum provided as an example in this text, they can also be graded based on performance and the proofs provided for each of the sections completed. An example grading form that might be used in conjunction with any practicum that you undertake can be found under part H of the photocopiable content of this chapter. This evaluation would also accompany bound submissions of the practicum that you would need to provide to your graduate program department office.

Depending upon the requirements of your graduate program, you may need to present five bound copies of the practicum to the department which will then lodge these with the university on your behalf, and house a copy in the department office. This will then see you officially complete all requirements of the program, allowing you to receive graduand status and to become eligible for the award of your certificate or degree. The practicum can then also serve as proof of your abilities to any prospective employee.

Summary

This chapter defined and explained the nature of a practicum, which is to assist you in developing confidence and competency while working alongside a teacher in a guided capacity. Although practicums may vary, there are some core components to each, and you were provided with an example that contains five tasks. Explanation of these tasks then went into detail regarding the time requirements and the logging of teaching, observing and evaluating lessons required, as well as aspects of completing professional development and engaging in lifelong learning.

Review

Content Quiz

Practicum

To help solidify some of the concepts introduced by this chapter the following multiple-choice and true or false quizzes might be helpful for you to undertake. So that you can check the accuracy of your responses, an answer key can be found following the quizzes.

Multiple-Choice

Circle **a**, **b**, or **c** for the answer that best completes the sentence presented in each question.

1. The purpose behind the practicum is to help pre-service and existing teachers …
   a) partner with others who can provide mentorship by directing their activities and giving them appropriate feedback on any work that they may perform.
   b) undertake original research and perform critical analysis of a topic while adhering to scholarly rigor.
   c) collect and evaluate student work that has been undertaken at key points throughout their academic career.

2. A practicum experience may involve …
   a) developing a rationalized reflective narrative that captures the scope, progress, and value of student learning, with student reflections supported by concrete evidence.
   b) a combination of class observations and providing classroom assistance as well as teaching classes, developing lesson plans, and providing supportive evidence of the ability to undertake lifelong learning.
   c) the undertaking of original research and performing critical analysis of a topic while adhering to scholarly rigor.

3. The role of your practicum advisor is to …
   a) help you solve unexpected academic problems, and resolve class issues that might impact your on academic path, while offering advice to keep you academically on track.
   b) provide mentorship, feedback, observation, and guidance during peer and clinical observations.
   c) ensure that you understand the tasks expected, that you have completed all tasks satisfactorily, and to give the practicum portfolio an evaluation.

4. The role of the practicum supervisory teacher is to …
   a) help you solve unexpected academic problems, and resolve class issues that might impact on your academic path, while offering advice to keep you academically on track.
   b) provide mentorship, feedback, observation, and guidance during peer and clinical observations.
   c) ensure that you understand the tasks expected, that you have completed all tasks satisfactorily, and to give the practicum portfolio an evaluation.

5. The purpose behind self-observation is to …
   a) gather feedback on your teaching practice for reflective purposes, and to evaluate if what you are doing as a teacher is successful.
   b) provide only the observer with the opportunity to enhance the quality of their teaching practice.
   c) Establish a process of practice where you can successfully observe others, and to offer mentorship, feedback, and guidance on others' teaching performance.

True or False

Circle **a** (true) if you think that the statement is correct, or **b** (false) if you think that the statement is incorrect.

1. Practicum requirements are standard across the educational field, and they do not vary from one academic institution to another or from one degree program to another.
   a) True.
   b) False.

2. Peer observation is all about being observed by a colleague or peer that your trust, so that they can offer you mentorship, feedback, and guidance on your teaching performance.
   a) True.
   b) False.

3. Peer observation provides teachers with the opportunity to share good practice methods, approaches, and techniques, while also sharing their thoughts on the practice of teaching and supporting each other in the development of teaching skills.
   a) True.
   b) False.

4. In the clinical observation process experienced teachers are relied upon as trusted colleagues rather than as evaluators.
   a) True.
   b) False.

5. A personal learning network or PLN can be defined as the way that you organize professional development and the system that you put in place to manage your own learning over time.
   a) True.
   b) False.

Quiz Answers
Practicum

Multiple-Choice		*True or False*	
1.	A	**1.**	F
2.	B	**2.**	T
3.	C	**3.**	T
4.	B	**4.**	T
5.	A	**5.**	T

Suggested Readings

Celce-Murcia, M. (Ed.). (2001). *Teaching English as a second or foreign language* (3rd ed.). Heinle and Heinle.

Crookes, G. (2003). *A practicum in TESOL: Professional development through teaching practice.* Cambridge University Press.

Kumaravadivelu, B. (2003). *Beyond methods: Microstrategies for language teaching.* Yale University Press.

Kumaravadivelu, B. (2012). *Language teacher education for a global society: A modular model for knowing, analyzing, recognizing, doing, and seeing.* Routledge.

Lynch, B., & Shaw, P. (2005). Portfolios, power, and ethics. *TESOL Quarterly, 39*(2), 263-297.

Richards, J., & Crookes, G. (1988). The practicum in TESOL. *TESOL Quarterly, 22*(1), 9-27.

Richards, J., & Lockhart, C. (1994). *Reflective teaching in second language classrooms.* Cambridge University Press.

Richards, J. & Renandya, W. (Eds.). (2002). *Methodology in language teaching: An anthology of current practice.* Cambridge University Press.

Scrivener, J. *Learning teaching: The essential guide to English language teaching* (3rd Ed.). MacMillan. [Chapter 16]

Ur, P. (2012). *A course in English language teaching* (2nd ed.). Cambridge University Press.

Woodward, T. (2001). *Planning lessons and courses.* Cambridge University Press.

Photocopiable Content

Practicum

This section of the chapter includes a variety of material that is free to photocopy. Use it to help you complete a practicum. It contains the following content provided under different parts from A through H.

Part A

A1. Practicum observation hours – Timesheet

Part B

B1. Self-reflection – Teaching logs
B2. Student appraisal form
B3. Self-evaluation checklist
B4. Self-reflection questions

Part C

C1.1 Observation worksheet 1a – Classroom snapshot 1 (Impressions)
C1.2 Observation worksheet 1b – Classroom snapshot 2 (Interactions)
C1.3 Observation worksheet 1c – Classroom snapshot 3 (What helps people learn?)
C1.4 Observation worksheet 1d – Classroom snapshot 4 (Errors and correction)
C1.5 Observation worksheet 1e – Classroom snapshot 5 (The learners)
C2. Observation worksheet 2 – Teachers and learners
C3. Observation worksheet 3 – Options and decisions
C4. Observation worksheet 4 – Thoughts, questions, and appropriation
C5. Observation worksheet 5 – Influencing the learning environment

Part D

D1. The observation process

Part E

E1. Pre-observation feedback

E2. Clinical observation form

Part F

F1. Lesson plan development and reflection guide

F2. Lesson plan structure general guide

Part G

G1. Professional development – Conference attendance

G2. Professional development – Conference presentation

G3. Professional development – Online participation

Part H

H1. Practicum evaluation sheet – Task requirements

A1. Practicum Observation Hours – Timesheet			
Date	**Class**	**Focus**	**Length**
(YYYY-MM-DD)	(Name and type of class, e.g., GTC23 – Sophomore Reading, English minors)	(Practicum stage, e.g., self-observation, peer observation, clinical supervision/peer observed)	(e.g., 60 minutes)
		Total self-observation hours:	
		Total peer observation hours:	
		Total clinical supervision hours:	
		TOTAL HOURS:	

Practicing teacher:

I, ______________________________, certify that the above hours are correct.

Signed ____.

Clinical supervisor/Peer observer

I, ____________________, certify that I have observed the person named above for the hours specified in this time sheet.

Signed ____.

Photocopiable Content - Practicum

B1. Self-Reflection – Teaching Logs

Name: **Type of class:**
Date: **Age:**
Number of students: **Level:**

1. Provide a brief explanation of the lesson and students (e.g., What are they working on during the lesson? What progress is being made to accomplish the learning objectives of the day?)

2. List the teaching techniques that you were able to use in the lesson, and why you found them to be especially useful.

3. Were you able to identify any individual student needs or issues during the class? If so, please list them.

4. What syllabus elements were incorporated into this lesson? How did you identify which are the most appropriate for your learners to concentrate upon during the class?

5. Did you use any supplementary resources during the lesson? If so, please list what you used.

6. Which teaching methods, approaches, or techniques did you use with students in this lesson? List each with a reason why you chose to employ it.

7. Did you have any problems with student behavior during the class? If so, list the steps that you used to overcome these problems.

8. Provide a brief summary of how you feel the lesson went, and what you might do differently if teaching the same material again?

9. Consider any other comments you might want to note regarding the lesson and make them here.

B2. Student Appraisal Form

Explanation: The purpose of this questionnaire is to provide the teacher with feedback on their teaching performance. Your feedback is important as it can help improve the lessons that you receive from your teacher. Please think carefully as you answer each question, and answer as honestly and as best as you can. Keep in mind that all of your answers will remain anonymous.

I have found that this teacher …	***Strongly disagree***	***Disagree***	***Neither***	***Agree***	***Strongly agree***
1. communicates class material clearly.	1	2	3	4	5
2. is well prepared for class.	1	2	3	4	5
3. organizes class time effectively.	1	2	3	4	5
4. stimulates my interest in the subject.	1	2	3	4	5
5. is responsive to student problems.	1	2	3	4	5
6. can teach well.	1	2	3	4	5

B3. Self-Evaluation – Checklist					
		A **No** answer means that improvement is possible. **N/A** means not applicable.	**Yes**	**No**	**N/A**
Language content	1	Did you teach any specific language items during your classes?			
	2	If so, did you find out how many students grasped the meaning?			
	3	Did enough students get the chance to re-use these target language items?			
	4	Did students use these language items to say anything meaningful?			
	5	Do students have a written record of new learning?			
Skills practice	1	Were you trying to practice one specific skill or a mixture of skills?			
	2	Were some tasks, or parts of tasks, appropriate for weak students and some for better ones?			
	3	Did students find the activities motivating?			
	4	Did most students receive some practice in the use of target skills?			
Correction	1	Did you concentrate on relevant points and avoid overcorrecting mistakes?			
	2	Did you only focus on students' communication abilities and ignore errors of form?			
	3	Was there a satisfactory level of accuracy in language practice?			
	4	If not, were you able to identify or provide a solution?			
	5	Did you provide students with scope for self- and peer-correction?			

		A **No** answer means that improvement is possible. **N/A** means not applicable.	**Yes**	**No**	**N/A**
Stages in lesson	**1**	Did you try to do too much or too little?			
	2	Could the activities have been better sequenced?			
Class management	**1**	Did you generally keep control of who spoke, and when (not too much calling out)?			
	2	Did you make sure some reluctant students (non-volunteers) participated?			
	3	Was there more student talk than teacher talk?			
	4	Did students speak English with each other?			
	5	Did you do anything to leave students with a feeling of achievement (e.g., use of exit tickets to evaluate, summarize, review)?			
Lesson structure	**1**	Did you include a variety of activities?			
	2	Were tasks and instructions clear to students?			
	3	Did you utilize visuals, realia, or other supplementary material?			
	4	Did you incorporate student experience, knowledge, and aspects of their own lives into the lesson?			

A **No** answer means that improvement is possible. **N/A** means not applicable.			Yes	No	N/A
New language items	1	Did you present new language items in an understandable way?			
	2	Did you provide comprehension checks for students?			
	3	Did you recycle vocabulary throughout the lesson?			
	4	Did you recycle vocabulary from previous lessons?			
	5	Did you ensure students recorded new vocabulary in a notebook or elsewhere?			
Skills practice	1	Did you focus on the participation of weak students?			
	2	Did you adjust the level of difficulty of tasks as required?			
	3	Did you provide repetition and mechanical practice for students?			
	4	Did you provide meaningful practice for students?			
	5	Did you ensure student-to-student work occurred?			
Class management	1	Did you have to nominate any students to speak?			
	2	Did you utilize non-volunteers?			
	3	Did you use student names?			
	4	Did you limit teacher talk time?			

B4. Self-Reflection – Questions

1. What was one great thing that you particularly noticed about your teaching?

2. What was one big weakness that you noticed regarding your teaching?

3. What was one thing that you really wanted to do or achieve with this class but could not do?

4. What is one reason why you could not do that one thing that you really wanted to do?

5. What aspect(s) of your teaching would you really like to keep and why?

6. What aspect(s) of your teaching would you particularly like to change and why?

7. What do you consider the most important thing that you have learned by completing this practicum task?

C1.1 Observation Worksheet 1a
Classroom Snapshot 1 (Impressions)

Obtain permission to visit a class for around 10–15 minutes. Your aim is to gain a general snapshot of what occurs. While you are in the room, answer the following questions. For the first few questions aim to be descriptive, but for the final question aim to answer more subjectively.

1. Describe how the learners are positioned (seated/standing) in the room.

2. Describe in general what is happening (e.g., 'an audio recording is being played, learners are listening for answers to fill in a blank on a worksheet')

3. Who is doing the speaking? Who is doing any other thing?

4. Describe a) the feeling; and b) the level of engagement in the room.

C1.2 Observation Worksheet 1b

Classroom Snapshot 2 (Interactions)

Obtain permission to go into a teacher's classroom for around 10–15 minutes. Your aim is to gain a snapshot of what is occurring in the lesson. Ask the instructor not to prepare any special activities for the time you will be observing. While in the room the aim is to consider speaking and interaction patterns.

1a. Who speaks?

Consider:

i. Who does the speaking?

____
____
____
____
____

ii. Who do they speak to?

____
____
____
____
____

iii. Who does not speak?

____
____
____
____
____

1b. The who speaks sketch

In the space below, sketch the classroom and mark the seating positions of students and the position of the instructor in the room (standing or sitting). Then, over a two-minute period at the start of the lesson, or any new activity, put a mark (e.g., a tick) next to anyone who speaks. Using different colored ink, repeat this during another one or two points in the lesson, and see how the results might differ.

2. Interaction patterns

In the space below, draw another sketch of the classroom layout. Then, choose a two-minute period during a whole-class speaking activity. Add arrows to the diagram to indicate who speaks to whom.

C1.3 Observation Worksheet 1c

Classroom Snapshot 3 (What helps people learn?)

Obtain permission to go into a teacher's classroom for around 10–15 minutes. While observing the classroom, the activities employed, the teacher, and the student interaction aim to answer:

- What can you identify occurring that establishes a good atmosphere for effective learning to occur?
- What can you identify that might be inhibiting any learning from occurring?

The Physical Classroom
Make notes regarding seating, sight lines, the board, the temperature, free space, lighting conditions, equipment, and so on.

The Activities
Make notes on the kind of activities employed by the instructor, the student involvement, and the balance of student and teacher interaction.

The Teacher
What personal qualities does the instructor have that you think are well suited to teaching)? What kind of rapport does the instructor possess with students? What kind of classroom atmosphere does this instructor generate? What do you think it would feel like to be a student of this instructor?

The Learners
How motivated are these students? Why? To what extent are they active participants in their own learning? To what extent are they expecting the instructor to do everything for them?

C1.4 Observation Worksheet 1d
Classroom Snapshot 4 (Errors and correction)

Obtain permission to go into a teacher's classroom for around 10–15 minutes. While observing, note down some student errors and how the instructor deals with them. Categorize each error (e.g., wrong tense, wrong phoneme, meaning unclear, and so on). Describe in detail what happens.

Examples

Error: I am agree. *Type of error:* unnecessary word.
Indication/correction: Teacher holds up three fingers (representing words of the sentence), throws away the middle finger. Student looks puzzled, then says the sentence again without the middle word. The teacher acknowledges this is correct with a smile and by saying, 'Good!'.
Error: Give me that pen. *Type of error:* Rude. *Indication/correction:* not commented upon or dealt with.

Considerations

Did anyone notice that there was an error? Who?
Did the teacher do anything?
Did the student do anything?
Did the other students do anything? Who?
Did anyone indicate that there was an error? Who?
Did anyone correct the error? Who?
How was it corrected?

Error:
Type of error:
Indication/correction:

Error:
Type of error:
Indication/correction:

Error:
Type of error:
Indication/correction:

C1.5 Observation Worksheet 1e
Classroom Snapshot 5 (The learners)

Obtain permission to go into a teacher's classroom for around 10–15 minutes. While observing, consider the lesson from the student's point of view. To do this, choose (secretly) one student to focus on and make notes about them below.

1. Choose a random two-minute period. Write a narrative description of what the student does.

2. Choose a random two-minute period. Write a narrative description of what you imagine the student is thinking or feeling.

3. Towards the end of the lesson write down what you think might be the student's description of what has happened in the lesson.

i. Did you enjoy the class?

ii. Did you learn anything from it?

iii. Did the teacher help you in anyway?

iv. Did you talk to the teacher or other students at all?

v. Did you expect anything to happen during the class that did not happen? (e.g., different activities used).

C2. Observation Worksheet 2
Teachers and Learners

Obtain permission to observe a teacher's class for a whole lesson. As you observe, decide if the statement on the left or right best fits the teacher and the learners, or is it somewhere in the middle.

The teacher				
Instructor often uses expressions (e.g., smiles).				*Instructor does not often use expressions.*
Instructor is too loud or too quiet.				*Instructor uses a natural conversational volume appropriate to the room.*
Instructor acts naturally (as they would outside the classroom).				*Instructor is distinctively 'teacherly'.*
Instructor speaks excessively.				*Instructor speaks very little.*
Instructions are clear.				*Instructions are unclear.*
Instructor makes mainly open-ended inquiries.				*Instructor makes mainly close-ended inquiries.*
Instructor comes across as impatient.				*Instructor comes across as patient.*
Clear dissemination of information, understood by learners.				*Information conveyed unclearly, misunderstood by learners.*
Instructor is oblivious to learner feedback throughout the lesson.				*Instructor notes learner feedback throughout the lesson.*
Instructor does not adjust to learner response.				*Instructor adjusts to learner response.*
Instructor works at own pace.				*Instructor works at learner pace.*

Comments on the instructor

The learners				
Generally engaged.				*Not generally engaged.*
Take a passive role.				*Take an active role.*
Mainly follow instructions.				*Remain largely anonymous.*
Balanced participation levels.				*One or two learners dominate.*
Comments on the learners				

C3. Observation Worksheet 3
Options and Decisions

Obtain permission to observe a teacher's class for a whole lesson. As you observe, consider aspects of classroom management. 'Classroom management' refers such things as the moment-to-moment decisions made by the teacher, as well as the actions that the instructor takes throughout a lesson when dealing with material and students, e.g., writing on the board, giving instructions, organizing the class into pairs or groups. For every decision made, there will have been other options that the teacher may not have chosen. For each of the following headings:

1. Note specific examples of classroom situations, and state how the instructor responded.
2. Note alternate options that the teacher might have adopted instead.

Example: Dealing with unexpected problems
Situation: A student arrives twelve minutes late.
Action: Teacher said 'hello'. (The student sat down quietly and asks what is going on in the class from their partner).
Other options: The instructor might have asked why the student arrived late. The instructor may have also pointed out the time to the student.

Student participation in lesson

Situation:

Action:

Other options:

Grouping of students, arrangement of seating

Situation:

Action:

Other options:

Set up of activities, instructions

Situation:

Action:

Other options:

Board use/layout; classroom equipment; visual aids; realia

Situation:

Action:

Other options:

Dealing with unexpected issues

Situation:

Action:

Other options:

Instructor's role and participation

Situation:

Action:

Other options:

Other notes concerning the lesson

C4. Observation Worksheet 4
Thoughts, Questions, and Appropriation

Obtain permission to observe a teacher's class for a whole lesson. As you observe, note a few things that you observe, and record your own thoughts, questions, or suggestions regarding them. Also note down several things that you consider worthy of appropriating (i.e., something you would like to borrow for use in your teaching – personal qualities, teaching skills and techniques, activities, classroom atmosphere). Finally, choose something that you feel that you would like to suggest for this teacher to change, or to use later in their teaching (e.g., a different way to deliver an activity).

During the lesson
I noticed …
I wondered …

During the lesson
I noticed …
I wondered …

During the lesson
I noticed …
I wanted to ask you …

Appropriated item
Description of the item …
I like this because …

Appropriated item
Description of the item …
I like this because …

Appropriated item
Description of item …
I like this because …

Suggestion
I'd like to suggest …
I think you will like this because …

C5. Observation Worksheet 5

Influencing the Learning Environment

Obtain permission to observe a teacher's class for a whole lesson. As you observe, consider some ways in which the teacher may influence what occurs during the lesson. Select four or five of the following aspects, and consider the teacher's role in regards to each.

Aspects of the learning environment	**Instructor role**
Classroom atmosphere	Does the teacher establish and maintain a friendly and engaging learning environment?
Organization	Does the teacher take an active role in how the materials, free space, and time on task is utilized throughout the lesson?
Encouragement and support, promoting participation	Does the teacher provide positive support, promote realistically achievable lesson goals, and a means for students to take on an active role in the classroom?
Promoting guided discovery	Does the teacher use elicitation techniques, (elicit answers, construct questions, offer partial examples, encourage hypotheses, and so on) that lead the students to their own conclusions or to use their own language?
Presenting content information	Does the instructor appropriately explain, lecture or answer student questions regarding specific learning content?
Provision of samples of language	Does the instructor provide appropriate target language exposure to students when providing instructions, comments, and answering questions, and so on?
Materials and tasks	Does the teacher use appropriate materials and tasks suitable for the teaching or practice of the language points being presented?
Monitoring	Does the instructor constantly monitor what is occurring throughout the lesson?

Aspects of the learning environment	Instructor role
Informative feedback	Does the instructor provide useable and understandable feedback that supports the learning process? (e.g., draw on peers to assist in providing information about any mistakes or errors made, provides information about language forms and/or uses, demonstrates how to perform a task in a different manner, suggests additional work for early finishers.)
Learning habits	Does the instructor provide a sense of a timed lesson that occurs seamlessly, and seems to provide a formless learning process?
Selecting and presenting	Does the instructor introduce content in ways that are manageable for learners, seeing them work effectively or do students end up struggling with it?
Structuring and sequencing	Does the instructor sequence activities appropriately, or allow students to help select an activity that they want and how they will complete it?
Authority	Does the instructor use their authority appropriately and effectively? (e.g., closing activities or discussions, requiring certain actions from individual students.)
Raising awareness	Does the instructor increase learning by encouraging the students to notice language points, mistakes/errors, new vocabulary, and so on?
Guidance and direction	Does the instructor use their knowledge and experience to best guide, direct, or counsel students?
Learner training	Does the instructor increase learner awareness regarding their own learning processes, and provide any means for developing them more effectively or efficiently?

Aspects of the learning environment	**Instructor role**
Democracy and personal responsibility	Does the instructor ensure that all students are treated equally, and that each is held accountable for their own learning/ participation in the lesson?
Natural motivation	Does the teacher encourage lessons to flow naturally, and encourage the continued use of language if it emerges spontaneously?

Aspect chosen	**Instructor role – comments**

Area 1:	

Area 2:	

Area 3:	

Area 4:	

Area 5:	

D1. The Observation Process

Pre-Observation Meeting

In order for observation to be effective, it is necessary to have consultations prior to the observation so that the observer has some background on the class. It also gives the person being observed a chance to provide some input into the observation. For these reasons then, it is a good idea to hold a pre-observation meeting and discuss:

- the time and place of the observation (which obviously should be arranged so as to minimize any potential impact on student learning),
- the status/history of the learning group (year/degree, level, any other significant information),
- the location of the class,
- how the lesson fits within the course/module/program,
- the aims and objectives of the specific lessons,
- learning outcomes (what students are intended to learn),
- potential difficulties or areas of concern (an opportunity for the observee to flag any specific areas that they would particularly appreciate feedback on),
- any specific focus for the observation, aside from those areas of concern (e.g., classroom management, questioning techniques),
- assessment instruments used, and
- any particular concerns that the observer might have in terms of confidentiality and feedback.

Preparing the Students

It can be disconcerting for students if someone else attends the class without warning. So, it is sensible to explain to learners that a colleague will be attending the class, that they will be there to help you review your teaching, and that they will not be playing a part in class proceedings.

Observing the Class

The observer should:

- be unobtrusive, i.e., not in the direct line of vision of the teacher or students, but able to view both,
- be discreet, e.g., not leap in to correct what may be an obvious error,
- focus upon the teaching and learning processes, rather than the content of the lesson,
- continuously check the level of interaction between teachers and students, and
- aim to gather evidence for later interpretation and discussion.

The Recording Process

Depending upon what stage of the practicum you are completing, the recording process for the observation will be different. For the purposes of this practicum, a number of pre-prepared forms have been provided to make things easier for the observer and the observee, although it is understood that observers often do feel constrained by these.

Checking with Students

At the end of the class, it can prove useful for an observer to check with students about how they felt the lesson went for them. This could be completed in a small group, taking the form of a short-structured session after the teacher has left. Aspects that the observer can bring up may include asking students for their opinions on the teaching and observation process, and their understanding of the material, i.e., learning outcomes. In a larger group (e.g., lecture), a few minutes of conversation with two or three students can at least give the observer a flavor of how the lesson has gone over for them.

Reflecting on the Teaching

The final part of the observation process is to reflect on the evidence gathered during the lesson. To this end, you will try to identify strengths and those areas in which colleagues or you may be encouraged to consider improvements.

E1. Pre-Observation Feedback Form

(to be completed before teaching a lesson and given to the observer)

Instructor:	Class:
Observer:	Level:
Date:	Time:

Teacher's Outline of Lesson to be Observed

1. **Specific aspects of the curriculum taught in the lesson**
   (e.g., competencies, learner objectives)

2. **Instructional strategies used in the lesson**
   (e.g., lecture, small group discussion, cooperative groups, technology integration, and why)

3. Learning activities
What learning activities will the students be engaged in?

4. Learning outcomes
How will lesson learning outcomes be achieved? How will you know if they have been achieved?

5. Specific performance areas/criteria
List anything specific that you want the observing teacher to look for or to comment on during the lesson.

6. **Student differences**
   How will you accommodate different learners, those at different levels, differentiated instruction, etc?

7. **Sample materials**
   Attach a copy of any additional content used during the lesson (e.g., handouts).

8. **Observer comments** (if any)

E2. Clinical Observation Form

Instructor: Class:
Observer: Level:
Date: Time:

1. **Aims and objectives**
   Were the aims and objectives of the lesson clearly explained or presented to students? Did the lesson have a clear focus?

2. **Appropriateness of materials**
   How appropriate were classroom activities in achieving the aims and objectives of the lesson? How effective was the content presented for helping students obtain the stated learning outcomes? Was the material/content provided to learners too much or too little for the lesson?

3. Organization of the lesson

How appropriate was the organization of the lesson?

4. Stimulating learner interest

To what extent was the instructor able to stimulate and sustain learner interest throughout the lesson?

5. Opportunities for learner participation

Did students have enough opportunities to participate in learning activities effectively?

6. **Use of teaching aids**
   How effectively were teaching aids (handouts, whiteboard use, and so on) utilized throughout the lesson?

7. **Explaining difficult concepts**
   To what extent was the instructor able to explain difficult concepts to learners?

8. **Effectiveness**
   Was the lesson effective? Why or why not?

9. Any other general observations

10. Observed instructor's response

F1. Lesson Plan Development and Reflection Guide

Rationale

The rationale behind the teaching process should be brief, and define any terminology from the literature that you may be using. It will ideally be based on your theory of teaching and learning or that expected by the school where the lesson is being provided. For example, a presentation, practice, production (PPP) approach will be used as part of a communicative language teaching lesson that employs total physical response as a means of teaching how to tell the time. PPP is being applied to move learners to understanding by presenting the material, helping them practice it, and then having them produce it using CLT to emphasize socialization and collaboration of students in pair and group work, while TPR is used to help engage young learners further with the content.

Learning context

Provide a description of your teaching and learning environment using the subheadings below.

- The Practitioner (years of teaching service, number of years in present position, what classes have been taught and to who and at what levels, usual teaching style).
- The Students (age range, gender, total number, practitioner perceptions [of the actual language level, learning styles, and classroom behavior of the students, differentiation requirements]).
- The School Situation (how many teachers/students, courses provided, location).
- The Classroom Context (length of lessons, kind of activities usually completed and why).

Materials and Resources

Describe in detail the materials and resources that you will use throughout the lesson using the subheadings below.

- Pre-Prepared Material (explain the nature of the material, usage, and any personal expenses required).
- In-Class Material.
- Homework/Follow-up Materials.
- Additional Supplementary Material.

Aims & Goals
Identify the aim(s) of the lesson (tied to the rationale in one or two clear statements).

Implementation
Detail the procedure(s)/method(s) of implementation taken by the instructor. (If you are using the lesson plan over several class periods then this could be outlined by stages such as: lesson 1 to lesson 5, or step 1 to step 5.)

Reflection: Outcomes and Implications
Provide brief commentary on the outcomes and implications of the lesson using the subheadings below:

- *Anticipated versus Actual outcome(s)* (what actually happened at the end of the day?, Did the project work or not [including to your satisfaction]?, What contribution did the use of tech provide over non-tech [if any]?, What major problems emerged?, What could solve those problems in the future?, What would you change next time you teach this lesson?)
- *Implications* (Where will this go in the future [both for the class/students and you]? Can you develop an action plan for the future?)

Lesson Structure
This consists of a detailed lesson plan, and one that can be constructed using the general guide on the following page. It is the actual plan that you would use to guide your lesson, and the one that could be handed to another teacher to follow if they had to teach the lesson on your behalf.

F2. Lesson Plan Structure General Guide

Teaching Context	
Levels of language proficiency and student maturity	Student language level, e.g., beginner, intermediate, advanced. Student age range, e.g., young learners, adults.
Lesson length	Time allotted for the class, e.g., 35-45 minutes.
Lesson topic	Major theme or focus of the lesson, e.g., numbers and time.
Objectives	Lesson aims, e.g., to teach students how to tell the time and date accurately.
Outcomes	Learning outcomes, e.g., students will be able to read analog and digital timepieces.
Relevant prior learning	Anything that students need to know before starting work on this lesson's content, e.g., students need to have completed Chapter Two of the book, and have previously met language associated with appointments, calendars, and timekeeping.

Teacher Preparation	
Hardware	Types of computer or peripherals required, e.g., USB sticks.
Software	Name of software used, e.g., Microsoft PowerPoint, Microsoft Word, Zoom.
Webpage links	Hyperlink to web resources, e.g., www.google.com.
Additional resources	Other necessary materials for the lesson, e.g., handouts, worksheets, textbooks.

Procedure

Review stage (if required: 5 minutes)

Objective: e.g., encourage the use of previously acquired language.

Teacher: Indicate what the teacher says and does.

Students: Provide expected examples of student behavior.

Warm-up stage (10 minutes)

Objective: e.g., introduce new concepts and language to students in a meaningful manner.

Teacher: Indicate what the teacher says and does.

Students: Provide expected examples of student behavior.

Main stage (20 minutes)

Objective: e.g., allow students to utilize technology to become familiar with and apply the concepts and language content introduced in the lesson.

Teacher: Indicate what the teacher says and does.

Students: Provide expected examples of student behavior.

Practice stage (15 minutes)

Objective: e.g., allow learners to utilize the skills and language that they are expected to acquire during the lesson in a practical way.

Teacher: Indicate what the teacher says and does.

Students: Provide expected examples of student behavior.

Lesson summation stage (10 minutes)

Objective: e.g., instructor reinforces the importance of language concepts and skills acquired, stating how they will be useful in forthcoming lessons.

Teacher: Indicate what the teacher says and does.

Students: Provide expected examples of student behavior.

Further Considerations	
Follow-up activities	Suggest material that can be applied in a follow-up class. Also, be ready with activities for students who complete their class work earlier than expected.
Contingency plan(s)	Always prepare an alternate teaching scenario in case of any problems. For example, a sudden power outage, or a timetabling issue that could make the assigned room unavailable.
Evaluation	*Teacher:* Reflect on what worked well, and what did not, and how you might deliver the lesson differently or improve upon it when running it again. *Students:* Indicate how you assess learners to determine if what they have learned throughout the lesson meets the learning objectives.
The board	Ideally, throughout the lesson, you will use the board in a specific way. Use this area to draw what will appear on the board, and how you might use the board throughout the lesson. (e.g., outcomes or points to cover on the far left – the lesson roadmap, new vocabulary and words introduced to students throughout the lesson on the right. The center part of the board may be reserved for core parts of the lesson at the top and the structures to be practiced or learned, with the area below for student use when being asked to write answers).

G1. Professional Development – Conference Attendance

Organization	Name of conference and organization.		
Topic	Name of the presentation.		
Date/Time	Date and time	**Number**	e.g., 1 of 3
Summary			

Learning Comment *(Identify anything new that you have learned from the presentation, this can be something academic (e.g., a new language learning theory) to anything practical (e.g., a new method, approach, or technique that you might like to employ with your learners).*

G2. Professional Development – Conference Presentation

Organization	*Name of conference and organization.*
Topic	*Name of the presentation.*
Date/Time	*Date and time.*
Abstract	*Insert copy of abstract here.*

Insert copy of presentation here.

Insert PowerPoint slides of your presentation here.

Insert certificate of presentation here.

G3. Professional Development – Online Participation

Organization *Name of the organization.*

Post Topic *Title of the post.*

Post Location *e.g., Facebook permalink, forum URL.*

Number *e.g., 1 of 3.*

Post *Insert the text of your post here.*

Replies *(Insert an example of replies to your post here).*

H1. Practicum Evaluation Sheet – Task Requirements	
Section and Evaluation	**Comments**
1. Layout and logs *Evaluation:*	
2. Self-observation, and critical reflection *Evaluation:*	
3. Peer observation, and evaluation *Evaluation:*	
4. Clinical supervision (observation by a peer) *Evaluation:*	
5. Pedagogy project (lesson plan development and implementation) *Evaluation:*	
6. Professional development and engagement (lifelong learning) *Evaluation:*	

Worksheets

1. Logs – minimum of five hours for each of the following

- ☐ Self-observation
- ☐ Peer observation
- ☐ Observation by a peer (clinical supervision)

2. Self-reflection, student appraisal, self-evaluation

- ☐ Self-reflection – Teaching logs
- ☐ Self-evaluation checklist
- ☐ Student appraisal forms
- ☐ Self-reflection questions

3a. Peer observation

- ☐ Observation worksheet 1a
- ☐ Observation worksheet 2
- ☐ Observation worksheet 1b
- ☐ Observation worksheet 3
- ☐ Observation worksheet 1c
- ☐ Observation worksheet 4
- ☐ Observation worksheet 1d
- ☐ Observation worksheet 5
- ☐ Observation worksheet 1e

3b. Clinical supervision

- ☐ Pre-observation feedback
- ☐ Clinical supervision

4. Pedagogy project

- ☐ Pedagogy project development
- ☐ Lesson plan

5. Professional development and engagement – lifelong learning

[One of]

- ☐ Conference attendance [certificate of attendance provided, along with summary and learning comments of at least three presentations attended]
- ☐ Conference presentation (including ppt/paper presented, and certificate of presentation)
- ☐ Online participation (posts to professional forums)

Worksheet Comments:

Summary Comments:

Grade:	**Date:**

Supervisor:	**Signature:**

PORTFOLIO

2. The Portfolio Project

Overview

The portfolio typically serves as a capstone project to courses such as a master's in TESOL and it is usually undertaken by those who do not wish to complete a thesis. It serves as a means for prospective and in-service teachers to showcase their learning, consider their competency as a classroom teacher, and engage in the reflection of their learning and of the coursework that they have competed while undertaking graduate study.

Learning Outcomes

1. Understand what constitutes a portfolio, and the importance of reflection in its development.
2. Know the role of the advisor in portfolio development, and the time requirements associated with its construction.
3. Gain an appreciation of the preparatory steps of portfolio development, and identify what constitutes as work product.
4. Discover the guiding aspects behind the reflection and selection of work products to include in a portfolio.
5. Contextualize how a portfolio may be evaluated.
6. Comprehend how a portfolio should be completed.
7. Gain insight into how a particular portfolio should be developed and completed for submission to one specific graduate program.

The Portfolio

Most commonly, portfolios are used to collect and evaluate students' work that has been undertaken at key points in their academic career. There is no single way to develop a portfolio, and many different types of portfolio exist. Nonetheless, the portfolio should consist of a rationalized reflective narrative that captures the scope, progress, and value of student learning, with student reflections supported by concrete evidence (i.e., work products). In any well-developed portfolio, students should not simply construct a scrapbook or collage of course assignments. Instead, they should be reflecting upon all the work that they have undertaken during a program of study, and begin to selectively organize their program work products (assignments, presentations, and so on) in a way that provides evidence of documented academic growth and pedagogical skill achievement. By its very nature then, portfolios are very individual, varying from one person to another, one department to another, and one institution to another. It is therefore important to become familiar with the portfolio that you are expected to develop where you are enrolled.

The Advisor

Your advisor will be available to help guide you in the completion of your portfolio, answering any questions that you may have about the process. In some programs, they may closely mentor the development of the portfolio, particularly if it is undertaken as part of a class project. It is also the responsibility of the advisor to perform a final check of your submission, ensuring that everything has been completed satisfactorily, prior to granting approval for it to be submitted to the graduate team. In the case of a portfolio, the submission is typically pass/fail, but it also may be a graded pass.

Time Requirements

The completion time for the portfolio can vary from one university to another. You may have one year (two semesters) in which to complete it, or you may be given one semester. It may be a part of your final class, or it may be an additional project that you need to complete.

Thc Portfolio Project

Preparation

It is never too early to begin collecting items that you may want to include in a portfolio. Steps to consider from the very first graduate class might be:

Filing. Establish a system that specifically focuses on your portfolio. This means keeping a duplicate set of the work that you have submitted to individual courses and storing these as a portfolio record set, thus ensuring that you not only have a series of content that will be easily accessible, but one that may also illustrate a clear developmental perspective. This process also serves to provide a backup of your work and would ideally be stored separately, such as on a cloud-based storage system rather than a hard drive.

Contemplating. Think about your teaching beliefs, strategies, and values, how these relate to the content studied throughout your graduate program, and how these could develop into a coherent statement of educational philosophy. It is this statement that can help guide your reflection and selection of work products from your portfolio record set.

Networking. Talk to other students, teachers, and faculty about their approaches to teaching. Such conversations can often help to stimulate your own reflective processes, allowing you to better articulate them.

Diary keeping. Write down your goals for professional development and determine how completing work throughout the graduate program can meet these goals.

Workshopping. Consider presenting at and/or attending symposiums and workshops to expand your professionalism and help develop those critical and reflective skills which can prepare you for lifelong learning as well as those that are required for portfolio development and completion. This will help to develop your educational philosophy and goals, the teaching methods and strategies that you may want to apply with learners, and also the activities that you later engage in to improve on your own teaching when leaving the graduate program. All of these are important to weave throughout any reflective narrative that is being developed in a portfolio.

Work Product Selection

There is a range of work products that need to be included within a portfolio. These include any material that you have developed as a student during your course of study, which may range from a conference, class, symposium, or workshop presentation; a literature review; an annotated bibliography; a research project; or a pedagogy project/lesson plan.

The selection of work products, as well as your reflection on them, will generally be guided by several factors including your teaching philosophy and goals, your current level of teaching experience and responsibility, the teaching methods and strategies that you employ, the activities that you undertake in order to improve on your teaching, and the goals that you have for the future.

Teaching philosophy and goals. This will typically prove to be the foundation on which your portfolio is built, guiding you in the selection of work products for final inclusion. A teaching philosophy generally aims to answer one main question: *why is it that you do what you do as a teacher?* You would typically try to develop an answer to this based on four elements:

- Beliefs about how student learning occurs.
- Beliefs about how teachers can best help students learn.
- The ways that you put into practice your beliefs concerning effective teaching and learning.
- The goals that you have for your students.

Teaching experiences and responsibilities. When considering these, you will need to think about the courses that you are currently teaching, the ones that you have taught in the past, and perhaps the ones that you aim to teach in the future. Teaching activities that you have engaged in outside of the classroom are also important to consider here, and this may include the counseling, advising, or mentoring of students as well as things like preparing, chaperoning, and taking students on excursions, field trips, or camps.

Teaching methods and strategies. This means providing those work products that support your teaching philosophy and goals, and clearly showing an understanding of how they are effective in meeting them.

Activities undertaken to improve teaching. As you develop the portfolio, your reflections will begin to illustrate what has worked, what did not, and why, and how those things might be improved or changed to improve your effectiveness as a teacher. Consider what could be lacking (i.e., what you have not done but what can be worthwhile trying). This can include reflecting on how you could have revised or completed assignments differently, or how you may have participated better in the program to improve on your teaching.

Future goals. The penultimate reflection of the portfolio will see you needing to consider how all of the above (and all of your selected work products) come together to show how you need or want to move forward as a teacher, and to also briefly outline the steps that you can take in order to accomplish these things.

The Importance of Reflection

The process of reflective organization involved in the construction of a portfolio should illustrate how you have acquired your professional knowledge, and the proficiencies that you have gained by completing the program of study in which you have been enrolled. In other words, the reflection process is important because it requires you to review all of your work products in order to discover, understand, and then communicate what, how, when, and why they have helped you engage in learning throughout your program of study.

Some questions that Zubizarreta (2008) suggests that could help guide reflection, particularly when considering material to include in a portfolio, are:

- What have I learned? Why did I learn?
- What difference has learning made in my intellectual, personal, and ethical development?
- Has my learning been connected and coherent?
- Has my learning been relevant, applicable, and practical?
- When, how, and why has my learning surprised me?
- What have been the proudest highlights of my learning? What are the disappointments?
- In what ways has my learning been valuable?
- How does what I have learned fit into a full, continual plan for learning?

Model Portfolio

The following tasks and portfolio layout, along with the accompanying submission and evaluation procedures presented, are those that are currently used by the TESOL-MALL graduate program at Woosong University in the Republic of Korea.

Portfolio Tasks

There is a total of five tasks to complete for the practicum outlined here. It is important that you complete each task to the best of your ability, and adhere to the specific layout that is expected. This layout involves the following:

1. an introductory reflection,
2. a teaching English to speakers of other languages (TESOL) component,

3. a multimedia assisted language learning (MALL) component,
4. a culture in English language teaching (CELT) component, and
5. a summary reflection.

Portfolio Layout

The layout of a portfolio is typically very specific. The example discussed here uses the following structure:

1. Title page,
2. Table of contents,
3. Introductory reflection (Task 1),
4. Content components (Tasks 2 to 4),
5. Summary reflection (Task 5),
6. Checklist and declaration.

Guidelines to help you prepare the portfolio can be found in the photocopiable content section of this chapter.

Title Page and Table of Contents

The cover page, or title page of the portfolio, will have a specific style that needs to be followed, and this will be set by the particular university that you attend. It will typically see you include your name and nationality, the semester and years that you have spent in study at the graduate school, your advisor's name, and the semester and the year of portfolio submission. A template may have been provided to you by your graduate program, and it is the guidelines and specifications in that document that your advisor will check to see if you have laid out the cover page accordingly. An example is presented in the photocopiable section of this chapter, followed by an example table of contents.

Task 1: Introductory Reflection

The first section of the portfolio, following the title and the table of contents, is the introductory reflection. In this section, you will reflect on the circumstances that brought you to study at the graduate level. You would highlight the expectations that you had at the start of the program, as well as what you hoped to learn and do. You will also briefly introduce the other sections of the portfolio. The introduction to the portfolio should be completed in around 500 words.

Task 2 to Task 4: TESOL, MALL, and CELT Components

Each of the components in these tasks should begin with a short description of what you now know to be the focus and content of the component. These reflections should consist of a paragraph or two, and be in the range of 150 to 300 words.

Then, for each of the TESOL, MALL, CELT components include a minimum of two work products, and keep in mind that a total of nine work products is required in total for the portfolio. It is therefore advisable to focus on selecting three work products for each component. A work product would include any material that you have developed as a student throughout your course of study, and this may range from a conference, class, symposium, or workshop presentation; a literature review; an annotated bibliography; a research project; a published paper; or a pedagogy project/lesson plan. Following each of your nine work products will be a reflection of that work product in the order of 150 to 300 words. Things that you might reflect on for each of these work products may be:

- Why did you choose this piece?
- How does this piece expand or change your understanding of TESOL/MALL/CELT, yourself, your students, or some other element of the teaching profession?
- How will you use this piece, and what have you learned from developing it that might help you in the future?

Task 5: Summary Reflection

This section will see you reflect on all the material that you collected for presentation in the portfolio. It will also provide a summary of how your career has or might be shaped as a result of graduate level study. In other words, how do your experiences at graduate school aid in your future career path? This question would also be answered by presenting and considering your teaching philosophy and goals, and it should be in the range of 500 words.

Checklist and Declaration

In addition to the five core sections of the portfolio, you will usually be presented with a checklist and a declaration to sign and date. The checklist is provided to ensure that you have completed all necessary components, reflections, and sections of the portfolio. Then, by signing the declaration, you are affirming that all content is your own work, and that it is free of plagiarism. The checklist and declaration are to be submitted as part of your portfolio, and an example is included in the photocopiable section of this chapter.

Submission

Prior to final submission, for each work product that you choose to include, and for each of the necessary reflections that you develop, consider the following:

- Have you selected, organized, and presented the work product in a way that brings the most compelling evidence into focus for the reader (often your portfolio advisor)?
- Does each work product serve a purpose by supporting the points that you have made in your reflection?
- Do the reflections, and the supporting work products, give the reader a sense of who you are as a teacher?

Once you are happy with how you have prepared your portfolio, and your advisor has approved it, you are able to sign the declaration and finalize the formatting of the work for submission. Often this involves providing a bound project, and a certain number of copies (such as five) to your program department who will house this with the graduate team, the national and university library, and the department office. It would be your responsibility to check when the final dates for submission occur in each semester, and how many copies are required. The submission will also be accompanied by your advisor's evaluation. All of these serve as proof of ability to yourself, your friends and family, and to any future employer.

Evaluation

Although the portfolio is typically pass/fail, each section may also be assessed individually following certain guidelines or criteria. An example of the evaluation criteria, and the evaluation form used by the TESOL-MALL graduate program at Woosong University can be seen in the photocopiable section of this chapter.

Summary

This chapter focused on the importance of a portfolio, and the place for reflection in its development. Also considered were the place of the advisor and the time requirements for portfolio submission. It outlines the basics of what is involved in developing a portfolio, with particular emphasis on the kind of work products that might be included as well as the need to contextualize teaching philosophy and goals, teaching methods and strategies, activities undertaken to improve teaching, and future aspirations within those reflections. An example portfolio, with the means used to evaluate and submit it to one particular graduate program, was then presented.

Review

Content Quiz

Portfolio

To help solidify some of the concepts introduced by this chapter the following multiple-choice and true or false quizzes might be helpful for you to undertake. So that you can check the accuracy of your responses, an answer key can be found following the quizzes.

Multiple-Choice

Circle **a**, **b**, or **c** for the answer that best completes the sentence presented in each question.

1. A number of work products may be required for your portfolio. An example of a range of work products includes …
   a) an activity photocopied from a textbook.
   b) a lesson plan that you have developed, taught, and evaluated.
   c) your professor's course syllabus and curriculum outline.

2. A choice of work products for a portfolio may be guided by …
   a) your teaching philosophy and goals.
   b) the demands of your advisor.
   c) what you have found in a textbook.

3. Networking will help you develop a portfolio because you can …
   a) find someone who can develop it for you.
   b) talk to other students, teachers, and faculty about their teaching, which will help you reflect on their approaches and come to articulate your own much better.
   c) Talk to other students, teachers, and faculty about their teaching, which will allow you to improve your academic ability.

4. Filing is an approach to use regarding your academic work and assignments. It may help in the development of a portfolio by …
   a) keeping you busy.
   b) collating all of your work as duplicates, giving you a backup of everything you have completed in a course.
   c) collating all of your work products in one handy place, allowing you to categorize them into different record sets.

5. A well-developed teaching philosophy is a statement that …
   a) will get you in trouble with a school principal or advisor if they do not agree with it.
   b) is only useful to include on a curriculum vitae when looking for work, and serves no practical purpose.
   c) can help guide your reflection and selection of work products from a portfolio record set.

True or False

Circle **a** (true) if you think that the statement is correct, or **b** (false) if you think that the statement is incorrect.

1. Most commonly, portfolios are used to collect and evaluate student work that has been undertaken at key points throughout their academic career.
   a) True.
   b) False.

2. It is not the job of your advisor to guide you in the completion of your portfolio, or answer any questions that you may have about the process.
   a) True.
   b) False.

3. The process of reflective organization involved in the construction of a portfolio should illustrate how students have acquired their professional knowledge and the proficiencies that they have gained by completing the program of study in which they are enrolled.
   a) True.
   b) False.

4. Workshopping or presenting at a conference during your graduate program will help you develop critical and reflective skills that can prepare you to develop a portfolio.
   a) True.
   b) False.

5. The reflective narrative of a portfolio should only consist of a developed teaching philosophy, illustrating a range of teaching methods and strategies as well as engaging activities, as it does not need to focus on any other aspects of a student teachers academic development.
   a) True.
   b) False.

Quiz Answers
Portfolio

Multiple-Choice		*True or False*	
1.	b	**1.**	T
2.	a	**2.**	F
3.	b	**3.**	T
4.	c	**4.**	T
5.	c	**5.**	F

Suggested Readings

Bullock, A., & Hawk, P. (2009). *Developing a teaching portfolio: A guide for preservice and practicing teachers,* (3rd ed.). Pearson.

Johnson, R., Mims-Cox, J., Doyle-Nichols, A. (2009). *Developing portfolios in education: A guide to reflection, inquiry, and Assessment,* (2nd ed.). Sage.

Kumaravadivelu, B. (2012). *Language teacher education for a global society: A modular model for knowing, analyzing, recognizing, doing, and seeing.* Routledge.

Lynch, B., & Shaw, P. (2005). Portfolios, power, and ethics. *TESOL Quarterly, 39*(2), 263-297.

Richards, J., & Lockhart, C. (1994). *Reflective teaching in second language classrooms.* Cambridge University Press.

Seldon, P., Miller, J., & Seldin., C. (2010). *The teaching portfolio: A practical guide to improved performance and promotion/tenure decisions,* (4th ed.). Jossey Bass.

Wyatt, R., & Looper, S. (2003*). So you have to have a portfolio: A teacher's guide to preparation and presentation.* Corwin.

Zubizarreta, J. (2008). The learning portfolio: A powerful idea for significant learning. *Idea Paper, 44,* 1-6.

Photocopiable Content
Portfolio

This section of the chapter includes a variety of material that is free to photocopy. Use it to help you complete a portfolio. It contains the following content:

- Portfolio checklist and declaration
- Portfolio title page
- Portfolio table of contents
- Portfolio guidelines
- Portfolio evaluation criteria
- Portfolio Evaluation Form

Portfolio Checklist and Declaration

Use this checklist to ensure that your portfolio submission is in good order. Then complete the declaration at the end of the page when you are ready to submit your portfolio for final evaluation. Include this section with your portfolio submission. The declaration should include your full name, as registered in the University system, your signature, and the date of your submission.

Cover Page

The portfolio cover page includes:

- ☐ Name.
- ☐ Nationality.
- ☐ Student number.
- ☐ Semester and years of study at TESOL-MALL.
- ☐ Advisor's name.
- ☐ Semester and year of submission.

Table of Contents

- ☐ Provides an outline of all of the items included in the portfolio.

Interior Sections

- ☐ All sections of the portfolio use appropriate headers, with page numbers at bottom center.

Sections included:

- ☐ Introductory reflection.
- ☐ TESOL – Teaching English to speakers of other languages component.
- ☐ MALL – Multimedia assisted language learning component.
- ☐ CELT – Culture in English language teaching component.
- ☐ Summary Reflection.

Introductory Reflection

- ☐ Introduces the portfolio sections and provides a program reflection in around 500 words.

Content Components – TESOL, MALL, and CELT

- ☐ Each of the three content components (TESOL, MALL, and CELT) begins with a short description of what you now know to be the focus and content of that component in a paragraph or two (between 150 and 300 words).
- ☐ Each of the three content components should contain *at least two* work products.
- ☐ Each work product type is clearly labeled.
- ☐ *At least five* different genres of work products are included.
- ☐ *A total of nine* work products are included.
- ☐ A reflection is provided after each work product (150~300 words for each reflection).

Summary Reflection

- ☐ Contains a summary reflection of around 500 words.

Submission

- ☐ I will prepare five (5) hard copies for submission to the TESOL-MALL Graduate Program, and one (1) for my advisor.

Declaration

I, ________________________, state that all work in this portfolio is my own. I am submitting this portfolio as my capstone project for the Master's of Arts (TESOL) at Woosong University.

Signature: ______________________________. **Date:** ___________.

Portfolio Title Page

PORTFOLIO

for the Master of Arts

Name
(Nationality)
Student Number
Semester, Year – Semester, Year

Advisor: Name

TESOL-MALL Graduate Program
Woosong University

Semester, Year

Portfolio Table of Contents

Outline all of the items that you have included in your portfolio.

Section

1. **Introduction**
   1a. Introductory Reflection – [500 words]

2. **TESOL – Teaching English to Speakers of Other Languages Coursework**
   2a. TESOL: Focus and Content [150~300 words]
   2b. Work Product 1 – [*name the type included*]
   2c. Reflection on Work Product 1 [150~300 words]
   2d. Work Product 2 – [*name the type included*]
   2e. Reflection on Work Product 2 [150~300 words]
   2f. Work Product 3 – [*name the type included*]
   2g. Reflection on Work Product 3 [150~300 words]

3. **MALL**
   2a. MALL: Focus and Content [150~300 words]
   2b. Work Product 4 – [*name the type included*]
   2c. Reflection on Work Product 4 [150~300 words]
   2de Work Product 5 – [*name the type included*]
   2e. Reflection on Work Product 5 [150~300 words]
   2f. Work Product 6 – [*name the type included*]
   2g. Reflection on Work Product 6 [150~300 words]

4. **CELT**
   4a. CELT: Focus and Content [150~300 words]
   4b. Work Product 7 – [*name the type included*]
   4c. Reflection on Work Product 7 [150~300 words]
   4de Work Product 8 – [*name the type included*]
   4e. Reflection on Work Product 8 [150~300 words]
   4f. Work Product 9 – [*name the type included*]
   4g. Reflection on Work Product 9 [150~300 words]

5. **Summary**
   5a. Summary Reflection [150~300 words]

6. **Declaration**
   6a. Checklist and Declaration [checked and signed]

Portfolio Guidelines

The following is a concise guide to the elements that constitute the portfolio.

Cover Page

The cover page must include your name (and nationality), the semester and years you have spent studying at the Graduate School of TESOL-MALL, your advisor's name, and the semester and year of submission.

Table of Contents

Outline all of the items that you have included in your portfolio.

Interior Sections

Label all sections of the portfolio using appropriate headers, with page numbers at bottom center.

Section Contents

Each coursework section should contain *at least two work products from each content component*. The three content components include courses that start with TESOL, MALL, and CELT, although any work product with a focus on the content of the component is suitable for inclusion (regardless of the course to which it was originally submitted). A *total of nine work products are required* for inclusion in the portfolio. *At least five different genres of work products* need to be included.

Sections include:

1. Introduction
2. TESOL – Teaching English to speakers of other languages components
3. MALL – Multimedia assisted language learning components
4. CELT – Culture in English language teaching components
5. Summary

Portfolio Sections

Introduction

The introduction section sees you reflect on the circumstances that brought you to TESOL-MALL, your expectations for the program, what you hoped to learn and do, and other aspects along those lines. You should also introduce the sections of your portfolio here [about 500 words].

TESOL/MALL/CELT Components

a) For each of the content components, begin with a short description of what you now know to be the focus and content of that component in a paragraph or two. [150 to 300 words].
b) After each work product in a content component, provide a reflection on that work product. [Each reflection will be between 150 and 300 words]. Consider reflection on at least the following.
    - Why did you choose this piece?
    - How did this piece expand/change your understanding of TESOL/MALL/CELT, yourself, your students, or some other element of the teaching profession?

Summary

For the summary reflection, summarize the materials that you have collected, and write about your future aspirations for TESOL, how you intend to reshape or expand your career, and how your experience in TESOL-MALL will aid you along that career path [about 500 words].

Portfolio Evaluation Criteria

Cover Page, Layout, and Table of Contents
All satisfactorily laid out according to the guidelines and specifications presented within the provided template.

Introductory Reflection
Experiences are reflected upon in terms of how they relate to the program, the student as a teacher, highlighting current and future professional expectations and workplace situations, and consists of around 500 words.

Content Components
The short descriptions detailing the focus and content of each strand are accurate, and concisely articulated in 150 to 300 words.

Work Product Types
All work products included in the portfolio are clearly identified. There should be a minimum of two work products per strand, a maximum of five work products of the one type, and a total of nine work products all together. At least five different genres of work product are included in the portfolio.

Work Product Reflections
All work product reflections are clearly identified and come after each work product type. Each reflection is between 150 and 300 words, and covers:

a) why the piece was selected for portfolio inclusion;
b) how the piece expanded or changed your understanding of TESOL/MALL/CELT, your students, or some other element of the teaching profession, and
c) how the piece may be used or learned from.

Summary Reflection
Adequately summarize in around 500 words the contents of the portfolio, identifying how the contents of the portfolio can contribute to your future aspirations, how study in the program has seen you reshape or expand on your career as an educator, and how program completion will lead to such outcomes.

Portfolio Evaluation Form

Student:	**Number:**

Section	**Evaluation**	**Comments**
Cover page		
Table of contents		
Introductory reflection		
TESOL component		
MALL component		
CELT component		
Summary reflection		
Required number of work products		

Summary Comments:

Grade:	**Date:**
Supervisor:	**Signature:**

THESIS

3. The Research Thesis

Overview

The thesis track in a master's graduate program typically consists of four basic components: successful completion of coursework, candidacy examination, the formation of a thesis committee and the writing and oral defense of a thesis project that follows a specific timeline. This track is also typically undertaken by those students who intend to go on to doctoral level studies or to engage in independent research on a topic of their own design. As such, the completion of a thesis as the capstone project to a degree serves as a means for prospective and in-service teachers to conduct an original study and perform critical analysis on a topic of their own interest.

Learning Outcomes

1. Understand the purpose behind writing a thesis, and the importance of developing an appropriate completion timeline.
2. Develop an appreciation for the role of advisors in master's programs, and understand the responsibilities of a student when undertaking a thesis.
3. Comprehend the importance of scholarly rigor and ethical considerations while gaining insight into what can constitute academic misconduct.
4. Gain insight into the purpose of the thesis proposal, its composition, and what to consider when creating one.
5. Become familiar with the thesis layout, the procedures of the defense, and what is involved with the binding and final submission of the thesis prior to graduating.

The Thesis Project

The purpose behind writing a thesis is for you to undertake original research, and to perform critical analysis of a topic while adhering to scholarly rigor. Your thesis manuscript should demonstrate the following abilities, and that you are able to:

- plan and carry out a research activity;
- correctly analyze the results of the research activity, and draw reasonable conclusions from the findings;

- develop a coherent written description of the research activity in a scholarly acceptable manner; and
- potentially deliver the research at a presentation or rework it for publication.

The steps to complete the thesis project typically involve finding and working with a thesis advisor, developing a thesis proposal, completing multiple drafts of the thesis prior to undertaking an oral defense, and then binding and submitting a final version of the thesis for submission to the university in a timely manner.

Completion Timeline

The completion time for a thesis may vary from one graduate program to another. You may have one year (two semesters) in which to complete it, or you may be given one semester (six months). It may be a part of your final class, or it may be an additional project that you need to complete. You will also be assigned a thesis advisor who will assist you in answering any questions that you may have while you work on the manuscript. An example *thesis track timeline (two-year degree, undertaking a six-month thesis)* can be found in the photocopiable section of this chapter.

Advisors

Academic Advisor

In most graduate programs, all master's degree students are assigned an initial advisor upon admission to a program. This academic advisor offers advice to students when they need it throughout the completion of their program. They may or may not become the student's thesis advisor.

Thesis Advisor

Your thesis advisor will typically have a specialization in either the topic that you are looking at completing or the research methodology that you will use to undertake the research. This advisor will be available to help guide you in the completion of your thesis, answer any questions that you may have about the process, and ensure that you have completed candidacy requirements, developed a proposal, completed an ethics form, and are ready to present a draft of your thesis manuscript to the thesis committee prior to defense. If you pass the defense, it will also be the responsibility of your thesis advisor to ensure that you understand any corrections that need to be made to the manuscript prior to final submission. The advisor will then perform a final check of the thesis manuscript, to ensure that everything has been completed satisfactorily, before allowing your thesis to go to binding.

Working with your thesis advisor. Ensure that you are able to schedule regular appointments with your thesis advisor. Provide work that has been spell-checked and proofread, and assume that you are not the only advisee that your advisor is working with, and that it may take up to two weeks for you to receive any feedback on your work. For an example of student responsibilities regarding the writing of a thesis, and working with an advisor, see the *listing of thesis student responsibilities* checklist in the photocopiable section of this chapter. Expect to write multiple drafts of each section of your thesis, and ensure that you are using the same revision system that your thesis advisor is using to review your work (e.g., the use of the track-changes feature in Microsoft Word).

Developing a Proposal

The purpose behind writing a thesis proposal is to demonstrate to your thesis advisor that you have:

- identified a specific problem on a certain topic to investigate;
- developed an organized plan that will allow you to collect, obtain, or work with appropriate data; and,
- identified a method of data analysis appropriate to the topic and nature of the study.

The research proposal should be written in a way that it describes what you will investigate, why it is important to investigate it, and the steps that you will follow in order to complete the thesis. An overview of what a thesis proposal might consider is laid out in the photocopiable section of this chapter as the *composition of a thesis proposal*. A *blank thesis proposal template* is also provided. While you develop the thesis proposal, it is important to cite any references that you rely on, and consider copyright issues as well as those involving ethics.

Ethical Considerations

Depending on the nature of your research, you will need to consider ethical issues and implications concerning research development and the way(s) in which you will conduct your research. Your responsibilities as a researcher are many and varied, and you have an ethical responsibility to safeguard those from whom you collect data as well as the data that you collect.

Provide information. Make the research aims clear to participants, and inform them of how the results will be used, and provide feedback to participants (including the opportunity for participants to verify the data collected about them).

Obtain permission. Written permission may be required, whether it be from participants or their guardians (especially from parents of school children); from principals (to carry out research at a school); and from teachers (allowing you to sit in on classes and observe students). Participants should also be made aware that they have the right to withdraw from the study at any time.

Privacy/Confidentiality. Provide a written guarantee of privacy and confidentiality to individuals and organizations from whom you collect data. Further, participants have the right to remain anonymous, and you will likely need to provide pseudonyms so that participants cannot be identified.

Consideration. Plan data collection so that there is as little disruption as possible for participants (e.g., no lengthy absences from class, or any considerable interruption of lessons). Cooperate with people where you conduct the research (e.g., determine ahead of time if you will sit in on a class to observe it, where you will sit, how and for what length of time you will record data, how you will be introduced, and so on).

Acknowledgements. The cooperation and contribution of all participants should be acknowledged in a way that retains confidentiality unless otherwise requested.

Necessities. It is also likely that you will need to gain ethical clearance from the university where you are undertaking your degree for which an example form is provided in the photocopiable section of this chapter as the *human research ethics application.*

Citation and Copyright

It is expected that you will be citing the literature at length in your thesis manuscript and by doing so from the time you start to develop your thesis proposal. This might include the findings from previous research, quotations from literary works, as well as that from surveys and other test instruments. You may either be quoting while you cite, or you may be providing the quote in your own words (paraphrasing). It is important that, in either case, you provide the correct citation. All citation references need to be included in the reference section, and adhere to a referencing system such as that of the American Psychological Association (APA).

In some cases, the copyright of particular material may be held by a corporation or an individual, and the rights to its use may need to be specifically acquired. You would need to provide proof of acquiring the right to use the material in an appendix to the thesis.

If you fail to cite work and present it as your own, or fail to gain the correct rights to the use of copyright material, then you may be held accountable for plagiarism or academic misconduct. These are both serious offenses in the realm of academia, and it may see you fail your thesis at best or receive an expulsion at worst.

Plagiarism

Many universities rely on plagiarism checking applications, and may also require students to run their manuscript (as well as their class assignments) through such software in order to produce an analysis of the work. Examples of websites that may be used for such purposes are Turnitin (https://www.turnitin.com) and Copykiller (https://www.copykiller.com). The level of plagiarism acceptable at universities may vary. An example of what may prove to be acceptable is listed in Table 3.1.

Plagiarism Acceptability Levels	
Level	**Acceptability Percent**
Secure	0 – 9
Caution	10 – 15
Suspicious	16 – 20
Risk	> 20

Figure 3.1 Plagiarism Levels

Depending on the results that you receive after analyzing your work (assignments, thesis, dissertation, and so on) you may need to rewrite elements, or provide a statement of why that level of plagiarism is acceptable. In particular, this may prove to be the case when submitting your thesis or dissertation for examination. You may be required to use a specific form in order to do this; see the *plagiarism analysis report* under photocopiable content for an example. You may also need to make a response after the plagiarism check.

If the level is *secure,* you may need to reexamine your manuscript carefully to ensure that all is in good order, and that it follows all of the appropriate ethical guidelines so that it can be submitted for grading/examination.

For the other levels, you should amend/revise the sections of the manuscript that have been flagged with the aim to lower the level to that of secure. If the level cannot be lowered, then a statement may need to be provided as to why this level of plagiarism is acceptable for the document that you will submit for grading/examination.

For the *risk* level, you may need to contact your course advisor or thesis supervisor for assistance in terms of reviewing the content and any steps forward. Any work submitted at this level is likely to automatically fail.

Thesis Layout

A handy reference guide for when you come to write a thesis, *a thesis cheat sheet,* is provided in the photocopiable section of this chapter. Although it does not aim to be comprehensive and to cover all types of thesis, it can serve as a reminder of what at the minimum may be required of you to include within each section of the thesis as you begin to write it up.

Keep in mind that there are a number of approaches to writing a thesis. These may involve qualitative or quantitative methods, or both in a mixed-methods study. This will see students conducting research projects that may involve anything from autoethnographic inquiry, to the comparison of groups and the running of tests, interviewing participants or using focus groups, through to project development and assessment. A generic sequential thesis layout has most or all of the following components.

Title Page

The title page will typically contain the name of your degree, your name, your advisor's name, and the year of thesis submission. Your graduate program will be able to provide you with the exact format to follow.

Signature Page

The signature page will contain the signatures of your oral defense committee members. It will list the committee chair, advisor, and the other members of the committee.

Abstract

The abstract is a summary of your study in very clear and plain writing. It should be no longer than half a page (try for no more than 300 words). State the research issues, the problem(s) that you want to examine, the way that you intend to conduct your research (meaning: with who, and how), what the outcome will be, and the goals and significance of your study. You may consider breaking the abstract down into the following:

Background: the shortest part which will outline what is already known about your topic and relate it to your research by detailing what is known about the subject and what the study intends to examine.

Methods: the second longest section of the abstract which will present enough information to understand what research was undertaken and how, with the significance of the research highlighted and rationalized.

Results: the most important part of the abstract, and it may be the longest as well as it provides details about the findings.

Conclusory remarks: the final sentences of the abstract which will serve to provide:

a) your take-home message,
b) additional findings or matters of importance, and
c) the real-world implications and significance of the findings to the field, the limitations of the study, and any future research possibilities.

Note that whatever appears in the abstract must also be present in the main body of the thesis. The abstract also needs to be read and understood independently of the thesis itself.

Definition of Terms

If your thesis requires definitions of terms, you may choose to highlight these on the abstract page, in the introduction, or in the glossary if there is one.

Acknowledgements

This page allows you to thank those who provided you with assistance and support throughout the completion of your thesis. You can also credit any companies that provided facilities free of charge for you to run interviews, testing, and so on. You may also add a dedication here if your graduate program does not allow for this on a separate page.

Introduction

Provide the purpose of the study. Follow this with justification of the study by clearly stating what makes it significant and why it is worthwhile to conduct, then provide the research questions. You may also need to include a definition of terms, and you can cover these either here or in a glossary, or list them under the abstract. It might also be applicable to mention any factors that you needed to control, those that were out of your control, and those that you assume are taken into consideration.

Background/Literature Review

A literature review should be developed to support the process and purpose of your study, and the conceptual model behind your study can be included here. Break down the literature review into important sub-topics relevant to your investigation, aim to explore the key concepts, theories, and studies, and identify key debates, controversies, and gaps in existing knowledge.

Methodology

This section will detail the methods that you will use in the study, and the rationale for using those particular methods over others. You would include information regarding participants, and the instruments that were developed or used to collect the research data. The reliability and validity of the instruments also need to be discussed and you will need to detail the procedures that you used so that another researcher would be able to replicate your study if needed. Describe any risks for the participants involved if there are any. A clear description of how the results are going to be analyzed also needs to be presented in this section of the thesis.

Findings

The findings need to be presented in the same order as you presented your research questions. You will need to provide all of the descriptive data that emerges from your analysis along with the results of the procedures that you used (e.g., statistical testing, coding of interviews), and offer a brief summary of the results with foundational interpretations of what the findings indicate.

Conclusion

Provide the inferences and implications of what the findings present, offering insight into what the study has done (and what it may not have done). Draw specific conclusions, and synthesize these with the literature/current knowledge in the field. Determine the limitations of the study, and provide recommendations for further research.

References

Provide a listing of all the material cited in the thesis in a scholarly format (e.g., APA citation style).

Glossary

If your thesis contains a large number of specific or unique terms, and/or a number of acronyms, it is important to detail them in a glossary section. List all the acronyms, terms, and key phrases in alphabetical order.

Appendices

Provide any additional data that is not included in the main thesis in this section. These may include ethics approval, survey examples, examples of thematic coding, examples of computer code, and so on.

The Thesis Defense

The Defense Committee

The thesis oral defense committee is responsible for reviewing your thesis manuscript. It is normally made up of a panel of three with one panel member being your thesis advisor, another, usually from your department, acting as the defense committee chair, and the third member either a member of faculty or an external examiner if required. The oral defense is pass/fail, and this is often the case for the thesis manuscript as well, although it might also be awarded a graded pass. Depending on your graduate program and the nature of the fail, you may have an opportunity to resubmit the manuscript for review by committee members in the following semester or be given an opportunity to resit the oral defense.

The Oral Defense

The oral defense is your opportunity to demonstrate that you are able to participate in a scholarly discussion regarding your research. The defense is typically one hour in length. It is advisable to plan for two hours, as you will need to arrive early to set up the room, and you will need to stay behind to engage in a debriefing session with your thesis advisor. You are welcome to bring guests to the defense if you require moral support, but you must obtain prior permission for this to occur from your thesis advisor. Otherwise, all guests will be required to leave once the proceedings begin.

Presentation. The defense will begin with you providing a short presentation regarding your research. This should be limited to around 15 minutes and it may involve PowerPoint or some other visual representation (e.g., the thesis conceptual model). The aim of the presentation is to provide a means of spring-boarding into a discussion regarding your research, and for the committee to see how well you understand the research that you have undertaken. You will need to do more than simply summarize your thesis. While preparing, consider answering questions like: *What led you to select this topic? What did you find particularly interesting or surprising as you investigated the topic? How is the topic of the thesis relevant to your current job or to future employment?*

Following your presentation, and perhaps some initial questions regarding the thesis by the defense committee, you may be asked to leave the room so that the committee members can discuss your presentation and the accompanying thesis draft.

Question and answer session. During the question and answer session of the oral defense, the thesis committee members will ask very direct questions regarding specific points about your thesis. Some may be very easy for you to answer, but others may prove very difficult. Remain calm, and take your time. If you do not understand a question, ask for clarification. Some of these sessions can be particularly difficult for students, and emotionally draining, because it is often the shortcomings of the thesis that are all brought to the fore over the many positives that may exist. Keep this in mind in order to help you get through this stage of the defense. The predominant aim of this session is to help make you aware not only of the positives of the thesis, but to draw attention to the negatives and to those aspects of the thesis that have fallen short. It is particularly important to do this, as the thesis committee members need to ensure by your responses that you are capable of addressing these issues in a redraft if necessary.

At the close of this session you will be asked to leave the room a second time, while the committee deliberates. You will then be called back to the room and informed if you have passed or failed the oral defense.

Evaluation

Your thesis, and defense of it, can be awarded one of several levels of evaluation. Each level will require a different response.

Passed defense. If your oral defense and thesis manuscript are both acceptable, and you address all questions posed by the defense committee in a satisfactory manner, then they will award a *pass for the defense*. You would then be able to proceed to bind the thesis, and officially submit it to the university.

Passed defense with minor revisions. If your oral defense is acceptable, you may still need to engage in some minor revisions before being able to prepare your manuscript for binding and official submission to the university, in which case you will be informed that you have been awarded *passed defense with minor revisions*.

Passed defense with major revisions. If your thesis manuscript has a number of shortcomings which you show that you are able to improve, then you will most likely be awarded *passed defense with major revisions*.

All of the revisions will need to be undertaken and reviewed by your thesis advisor prior to being allowed to submit the final version of your thesis to the university for binding.

Failed the defense. If the thesis manuscript is academically unsatisfactory (e.g., contains plagiarism), and/or you were unable to discuss your research adequately (i.e., indicating that you may not have written the manuscript), then you will not pass the oral defense. Additionally, if the manuscript has an excessive amount of inconsistencies or lacks academic rigor, and you are unable to demonstrate how the manuscript can be salvaged, then the oral defense will be awarded a *fail*. In any of these cases, the committee will come to a unanimous decision. They will then determine if and/or how you might address any shortcomings, and provide a timeline for you to do so. If permitted by the defense committee, you would then be able to undertake the oral defense a second time. The second defense will have the same guidelines as the first, with the oral defense allowed to be repeated only once.

Defense Debrief

After the oral defense you will meet with your thesis advisor. The thesis advisor will go over the decision made by the defense committee, ensuring that you understand it. They will then inform you of the next steps. If passing the defense this often means that they will help you understand all of the revisions that you need to perform, and set you a deadline to complete them. You will then provide a final draft of the manuscript for your advisor to review. If all is in order you will be granted approval to prepare the thesis for binding, and permission to ask the defense committee members to sign the signature page of the thesis. If failing the defense, the thesis advisor will help you understand why, and what you need to do in the timeframe provided in order to retake the oral defense if that is an option available to you.

Binding and Final Submission

Once you have passed the oral defense and made any required corrections to the thesis manuscript, your thesis advisor will perform a final check of the document. You may need to perform additional revisions before being permitted to officially submit your thesis to the university, and you will then need to work with the graduate program administrative assistants to adhere to all the requirements for this to occur (e.g., completing appropriate documentation and lodging the correct forms at the right times). Keep in mind that it will usually be your responsibility to check when the final dates for submission occur each semester, and how many copies of the thesis will be required. Depending on the graduate program that you are enrolled in, up to seven (7) copies of your thesis may be required, and they will go to such places as the university library, the national library, and to your thesis advisor. You will, at this stage, also be ready to format the thesis according to the university and/or government guidelines that are required. After formatting the document, it can then be printed and professionally bound for final submission to the university. Many universities require you to work with a particular print shop for this, and the administrative assistants of the graduate program in which you are enrolled will advise you accordingly. The bound copies serve as a record of your capability to perform research, and depending on the nature and quality of your material you may wish to rework it for journal article publication.

Summary

This chapter presented the rationale behind the writing of a thesis, and the need to follow a strict completion timeline. The role of advisors and students in the development of a thesis was also uncovered, as was the critical need to consider ethical implications when undertaking research. Scholarly rigor and academic misconduct were also discussed, along with what constitutes a thesis proposal. The typical sequential style thesis layout was then presented, along with stages of a typical oral defense, and the means of finalizing the thesis project for formal submission.

Review

Content Quiz

Thesis

To help solidify some of the concepts introduced by this chapter the following multiple-choice and true or false quizzes might be helpful for you to undertake. So that you can check the accuracy of your responses, an answer key can be found following the quizzes.

Multiple-Choice

Circle **a**, **b**, or **c** for the answer that best completes the sentence presented in each question.

1. The purpose of the title page of a thesis is to …
   a) present student academic information (e.g., name, student number, advisor name, name of degree, semester and year of submission).
   b) thank any of those who may have aided or supported you throughout the completion of your thesis.
   c) illustrate that the oral defense has been passed, and who comprised the thesis defense committee.

2. The purpose of the acknowledgements section of a thesis is to …
   a) present student academic information (e.g., name, student number, advisor name, name of degree, semester and year of submission).
   b) thank any of those who may have aided or supported you throughout the completion of your thesis.
   c) illustrate that the oral defense has been passed, and who comprised the thesis defense committee.

3. The purpose of the signature page of a thesis is to …
   a) present student academic information (e.g., name, student number, advisor name, name of degree, semester and year of submission).
   b) thank any of those who may have aided or supported you throughout the completion of your thesis.
   c) illustrate that the oral defense has been passed, and who comprised the thesis defense committee.

4. The purpose of the abstract of a thesis is to …
   a) illustrate that the oral defense has been passed, and who comprised the thesis defense committee.
   b) deliver a summary of your study in very clear and plain writing.
   c) compare and critique those studies that are most relevant to the research problem that you are investigating.

5. The purpose of the introduction section of a thesis is to …
   a) provide the purpose, justification, significance, and the rationale of what will be investigated.
   b) deliver a summary of your study in very clear and plain writing.
   c) compare and critique those studies that are most relevant to the research problem that you are investigating.

6. The purpose of the literature review section of a thesis is to …
   a) provide the purpose, justification, significance, and the rationale of what will be investigated.
   b) detail the methods and analysis applied to the study, along with the rationale for using those particular methods instead of others, while also discussing characteristics of the participants and the risks to them, the research instruments developed/employed, and the context of the study so that it can be replicated.
   c) compare and critique those studies that are most relevant to the research problem that you are investigating.

7. The purpose of the methodology section of a thesis is to …
   a) detail the methods and analysis applied to the study, along with the rationale for using those particular methods instead of others, while also discussing characteristics of the participants and the risks to them, the research instruments developed/employed, and the context of the study so that it can be replicated.
   b) compare and critique those studies most relevant to the research problem that you are investigating.
   c) provide all of the descriptive data that emerges from your analysis along with the results of the procedures that you used (e.g., statistical testing, coding of interviews), and offer a brief summary of the results with foundational interpretations.

8. The purpose of the findings section of a thesis is to …

a) detail the methods and analysis applied to the study, along with the rationale for using those particular methods instead of others, while also discussing characteristics of the participants and the risks to them, the research instruments developed/employed, and the context of the study so that it can be replicated.

b) provide all of the descriptive data that emerges from your analysis along with the results of the procedures that you used (e.g., statistical testing, coding of interviews), and offer a brief summary of the results with foundational interpretations.

c) present specific deductions, defining research limitations and providing recommendations for the future.

9. The purpose of the conclusion to a thesis is to …

a) present specific deductions, defining research limitations and providing recommendations for the future.

b) provide all of the descriptive data that emerges from your analysis along with the results of the procedures that you used (e.g., statistical testing, coding of interviews), and offer a brief summary of the results with foundational interpretations.

c) provide a listing of all the material cited in the thesis in a scholarly format.

10. The purpose of the references section of a thesis is to …

a) provide any additional data not included in the main thesis.

b) provide, in alphabetical order, a listing of all of the acronyms, terms, and key phrases used throughout the thesis.

c) provide a listing of all the material cited in the thesis in a scholarly manner.

11. The purpose of the glossary to a thesis is to …

a) provide any additional data that is not included in the main thesis.

b) provide, in alphabetical order, a listing of all of the acronyms, terms, and key phrases used throughout the thesis.

c) provide a listing of all the material cited in the thesis in a scholarly format.

12. The purpose of the appendix of a thesis is to …

a) provide any additional data that is not included in the main thesis.

b) provide, in alphabetical order, a listing of all of the acronyms, terms, and key phrases used throughout the thesis.

c) provide a listing of all the material cited in the thesis in a scholarly manner.

13. The thesis oral defense committee is responsible for …

a) chatting with you for an hour about your thesis manuscript.

b) reviewing your academic and research skills along you're your development of the thesis manuscript.

c) reviewing the spelling and grammar found in the thesis manuscript and to assess your citation use.

14. The thesis oral defense is your opportunity to …

a) chat with faculty members for an hour about your thesis manuscript.

b) demonstrate that you are able to participate in a scholarly discussion regarding your research.

c) defend all of the choices that you made while in graduate school.

15. The aim of the thesis oral defense presentation is to …

a) provide a means of spring-boarding into a discussion regarding your research, and for the committee to see how well you understand the research that you have undertaken.

b) provide some entertainment to thesis defense committee members.

c) take up time as the defense has to be an hour in length.

16. The aim of the question and answer session of a thesis oral defense is to …

a) point out all of the thesis manuscript shortcomings.

b) try and make the student cry.

c) determine if the candidate is capable of addressing any issues in the thesis manuscript and is able to redraft it in a timely manner for final binding and submission.

17. Passing the thesis oral defense often means that you ...
  a) will likely have a number of revisions to perform, and have a deadline in which to complete them, before being allowed to submit the thesis manuscript for binding.
  b) can throw a party to celebrate and then relax for the rest of semester, as the office assistants can now deal with the manuscript.
  c) feel a sense of accomplishment in completing the first draft of your thesis, and that you are able to now hand it over to the office assistants to deal with the binding process.

18. If you fail the thesis defense ...
  a) your dreams of graduating are over.
  b) your thesis advisor will help you understand why, and what you need to do in the timeframe provided in order to retake the oral defense if possible.
  c) you will not be able to retake the defense, and will need to be moved to the portfolio track for degree completion.

19. When binding the thesis ...
  a) many universities require you to work with a particular print shop.
  b) the graduate program office assistants will do everything for you.
  c) you can print it off at home and submit in a clear folder.

True or False

Circle **a** (true) if you think that the statement is correct, or **b** (false) if you think that the statement is incorrect.

1. The purpose behind writing a thesis is for you to undertake original research, and to perform critical analysis of a topic while adhering to scholarly rigor.
   a) True.
   b) False.

2. The steps to complete the thesis project typically involve finding and working with a thesis advisor, developing a thesis proposal, completing multiple drafts of the thesis prior to undertaking an oral defense, and then binding and submitting a final version of the thesis for submission to the university in a timely manner.
   a) True.
   b) False.

3. The role of the academic advisor is to supervise the progress of a college or university student as they undertake thesis research.
   a) True.
   b) False.

4. The role of the thesis advisor is to help students solve unexpected academic problems, resolve any class issues that might impact on their academic path, while also offering advice to keep students scholastically on track.
   a) True.
   b) False.

5. It is important to use the same revision system that your thesis advisor is using to review your work (e.g., the use of the track-changes feature in Microsoft Word).
   a) True.
   b) False.

6. The research proposal should be written in a way that describes what you will investigate, why it is important to investigate it, and the steps that you will follow in order to complete such an investigation.
   a) True.
   b) False.

7. Researchers have an ethical responsibility to safeguard those who they collect data from as well as the data that they collect.
   a) True.
   b) False.

8. It is important to make the research aims clear to participants, and inform them of how the results will be used.
   a) True.
   b) False.

9. It is important to provide feedback to participants (including the opportunity for participants to verify the data that is collected about them).
   a) True.
   b) False.

10. Written permission to participate in a study may be required for some participants (e.g., from a child's parent or guardian, from the principal, or from the teacher being observed).
    a) True.
    b) False.

11. Participants in a study should be made aware that they have the right to withdraw from the study at any time.
    a) True.
    b) False.

12. It is not necessary to provide a written guarantee of privacy and confidentiality to individuals and organizations from whom you collect data.
    a) True.
    b) False.

13. Participants may have the right to remain anonymous, and you will likely need to provide pseudonyms so that participants cannot be identified from your study.
    a) True.
    b) False.

14. The cooperation and contribution of all participants should be acknowledged in a way that retains confidentiality unless otherwise requested.
    a) True.
    b) False.

15. Prior to engaging in any thesis research, you may need to gain ethical clearance from the university where you are undertaking your degree.
    a) True.
    b) False.

16. There is no need to include all in-text citations in full within the reference section.
    a) True.
    b) False.

17. It is important to adhere to a consistent referencing system throughout the thesis. (e.g., APA style).
    a) True.
    b) False.

18. If you fail to cite work and present it as your own, or fail to gain the correct rights to the use of copyright material, then you may be held accountable for plagiarism or academic misconduct.
    a) True.
    b) False.

19. There are a number of approaches to writing a thesis. These may involve qualitative or quantitative methods, or both in a mixed-methods study.
    a) True.
    b) False.

Quiz Answers
Thesis

Multiple-Choice		*True or False*	
1.	A	**1.**	T
2.	B	**2.**	T
3.	C	**3.**	F
4.	B	**4.**	F
5.	A	**5.**	T
6.	C	**6.**	T
7.	A	**7.**	T
8.	B	**8.**	T
9.	A	**9.**	T
10.	C	**10.**	T
11.	B	**11.**	T
12.	A	**12.**	F
13.	B	**13.**	F
14.	B	**14.**	T
15.	A	**15.**	T
16.	C	**16.**	F
17.	A	**17.**	T
18.	B	**18.**	T
19.	A	**19.**	T

Suggested Readings

Celce-Murcia, M. (Ed.). (2001). *Teaching English as a second or foreign language* (3rd ed.). Heinle and Heinle.

Crookes, G. (2003). *A practicum in TESOL: Professional development through teaching practice.* Cambridge University Press.

Fraenkel, J., Wallen, N., & Hyun, H. (2018). *How to design and evaluate research in education,* (10th ed.). McGraw-Hill Education.

Joyner, R., Rouse, W., & Glatthorn, A. (2018). *Writing the winning thesis or dissertation: A step-by-step guide,* (4th ed.). Corwin.

Kornuta, H., & Germaine, R. (2019). *A concise guide to writing a thesis or dissertation: Educational research and beyond* (2nd ed.). Routledge.

Kumaravadivelu, B. (2003). Beyond *methods: Microstrategies for language teaching.* Yale University Press.

Kumaravadivelu, B. (2012). *Language teacher education for a global society: A modular model for knowing, analyzing, recognizing, doing, and seeing.* Routledge.

Lynch, B., & Shaw, P. (2005). Portfolios, power, and ethics. *TESOL Quarterly 39*(2), 263-297.

Rennie, L., & Gribble, J. (2006). *A guide to preparing your application for candidacy,* (Rev. ed.). Curtin University of Technology.

Richards, J., & Crookes, G. (1988). The practicum in TESOL. *TESOL Quarterly, 22*(1), 9-27.

Richards, J., & Lockhart, C. (1994). *Reflective teaching in second language classrooms.* Cambridge University Press.

Richards, J. & Renandya, W. (Eds.). (2002). *Methodology in language teaching: An anthology of current practice.* Cambridge University Press.

Scrivener, J. (2005). *Learning teaching: The essential guide to English language teaching* (3rd Ed.). MacMillan. [Chapter 16]

Ur, P. (2012). *A course in English language teaching* (2nd ed.). Cambridge University Press.

Woodward, T. (2001). *Planning lessons and courses.* Cambridge University Press.

Photocopiable Content

Thesis

This section of the chapter includes a variety of material that is free to photocopy. Use it to help you complete a thesis. It contains the following content:

- Thesis track timeline (two-year degree with six-month thesis)
- Listing of thesis student responsibilities
- Composition of a thesis proposal
- Blank thesis proposal template
- Human research ethics application
- Sample participant consent form
- Plagiarism analysis report
- Thesis cheat sheet

Thesis Track Timeline
(two-year degree program with six-month thesis)

First Year

Semester One

- Register for classes.
- Begin coursework.
- Meet initial academic advisor.

Summer/Winter Break

- Undertake readings for semester two classes.

Semester Two

- Continue with coursework.
- Meet with advisor as necessary.

Second Year

Semester Three

- Continue with coursework.
- Decide if you will complete a portfolio or thesis.
- If deciding upon thesis, meet with your thesis advisor.
- Decide on a preliminary topic for your thesis.
- Develop a thesis proposal and conceptual model.
- Complete the HREA (Human Research Ethics Application) form.
- Finalize members of the defense committee.

Summer/Winter Break

- Undertake readings for semester four classes.
- Finalize the literature review section of the thesis.
- Complete the methodology section of the thesis.
- Undertake any field work and data collection.
- Collate the data and begin analysis.

Semester Four (and Five if required)

- Complete program coursework.
- Finalize the discussion section of the thesis.
- Develop a conclusion and then introduction for the thesis, along with an abstract and a table of contents.
- Prepare the first draft of thesis that is to go to the defense committee.
- Prepare for the thesis defense.
- With advisor approval, distribute the first draft of your thesis to defense committee members.
- Sit for the oral defense of your thesis.
- Revise the thesis as required by the thesis defense committee.
- Submit the revisions as a final draft of your thesis to your advisor for review.
- After final approval from your thesis advisor, follow the graduate program procedures for submission of the thesis to the university.

Listing of Thesis Student Responsibilities

- ☐ I believe that my coursework writing experiences have enabled me to become familiar with how to write a research paper. If my advisor finds that this is not the case, I understand that I must put aside my thesis and first become familiar with the process of thesis writing before I can continue. (This might even entail enrolling in an approved writing course and/or needing more than one semester to write my thesis). It might also mean changing to the portfolio track (if that option is available to me).
- ☐ I understand that it is my responsibility to focus on form, and that my advisor is responsible for focusing on the content and assisting with developing an appropriate structure for the thesis. (e.g., my advisor should not be showing me how to use APA style, MS Word, or graphic aids. However, my advisor will notify me if the layout, the content of the tables or the thesis needs adjusting).
- ☐ I will make appointments to see my advisor during his/her regularly scheduled office hours whenever possible. I understand that this is why the university arranges for professors to have and maintain office hours.
- ☐ I do not expect my advisor to schedule special times to meet with me at my convenience; rather, I recognize my obligation to schedule appointments which are in all instances mutually agreed upon. Should I need to postpone or cancel an appointment, I will try within reasonable limits to provide my advisor with advance notice.
- ☐ I understand that it is also my obligation to arrange an agenda for scheduled meetings with mutual consent at least 5 days prior to the appointed date.
- ☐ I understand that it is my responsibility to provide specific updates to my advisor regarding the progress of my thesis, and to do so on a weekly basis, or as my advisor deems necessary.
- ☐ I understand that I must provide email documents/material to my advisor at least 5 days in advance of the receipt of hardcopies of sections of the thesis, unless my advisor waives this requirement.

- ☐ I understand that I should follow the research plan that my advisor and I have drawn up regarding my thesis, and that this research plan needs to be completed by the end of my third semester of study in the program. Any major modifications to this plan must be made in consultation with my advisor according to a mutually agreed upon and reasonable timetable for completion.
- ☐ I understand that, as a thesis student, I must make certain sacrifices, and that this includes working on my literature review and developing research instruments during summer and/or winter intersessions and that I will have to make a serious time commitment (including evenings, weekends, and holidays) if I intend to complete my thesis in a single semester.
- ☐ I understand that if I have neglected to prepare a study plan and thesis topic in conjunction with my supervisor in my third semester of study that I will need to do this as part of the thesis research course. Accordingly, I will then need to take advanced thesis research in a fifth semester and work on my thesis over two semesters and any intersessions.
- ☐ I understand that my advisor is assisting me voluntarily, and I need to respect the time and effort that they undertake to help me in the thesis writing process.
- ☐ I should consider all changes and recommendations offered, and understand that by ignoring any recommendations, I could fail my thesis defense, or I will need to resubmit the thesis in a subsequent semester.
- ☐ I have obtained and read the information on capstone projects prepared by the department faculty.

As a thesis student in the TESOL-MALL graduate program, I have read the above and by signing below, I indicate that I will honor my obligations and meet my responsibilities as outlined.

________________	________________	________
Thesis Student Signature	Thesis Advisor Signature	Date

Composition of a Thesis Proposal

Title Page

The thesis proposal title page may vary from one graduate program to another, but it should include your name and student number, your proposed thesis title, the name of your thesis advisor, the semester and year that you are lodging the proposal with your advisor, and the name of your graduate program.

Thesis Title

Your proposed title will be short (certainly less than 20 words, but aim for 15), and will attempt to accurately describe the research problem. The title needs to be as close as possible to the final title of your thesis.

Abstract

At this stage, you will need to develop a working abstract, and this document can help prepare the content of that abstract. State the research issues, the problem(s) that you want to examine, the way that you intend to conduct your research (meaning with who and how), what you think the outcome will be, as well as the goals and significance of your study. The abstract is a summary of your study (at this stage, the thesis proposal) in very clear and plain writing. It should be no longer than half a page (try for no more than 300 words).

Definition of Terms

If you need to define any specific terms used throughout the thesis you would go into detail regarding these here. However, you might instead prefer to include them in a glossary or incorporate them into another area of the thesis such as the introduction or the literature review.

Introduction

In this section, the research problem is outlined (what your research will aim to find out). This section must contain sufficient information to inform your advisor of what your thesis research will be about, and specifically what aspects your study will address. At a minimum, aim to consider providing a brief overview of the reason for your investigation, including the goals of your study and why these aims are significant or important. You should provide information under the following sub-headings:

Background and Context. Outline the topic and scope of the research to situate the reader.

Research Problem. Describe in detail the practical or theoretical research problem that you want to investigate or address. Consider what current literature knows about the issue here, and detail what is lacking from the literature. In other words, develop your research niche.

Significance. Indicate the relevance and importance of the research (i.e., how it adds to knowledge or makes an original contribution to knowledge). Clarify what new insights you will be able to contribute to the literature, to whom these insights are relevant, and why the research questions are worth asking, providing a summary of why and how the goals and aims of your thesis are significant and important. Indicate:

- how the results from your research could be used to help the target population;
- why the results could be important for other people in your field and how they might be used; and
- how the results could be important for other researchers.

You may wish to break the significance into two sections, practical implications and theoretical implications.

Practical implications. Will your findings help improve a process, inform policy, or make a case for concrete change?

Theoretical implications. Will your work help strengthen a theory or model, challenge current assumptions, or create a basis for further research?

Research Questions. State very clearly the research question and any subsidiary questions. (You should have at least three questions, but you may need to write down as many as you can to help you consider all aspects of the problem that you are investigating).

Photocopiable Content – Thesis

Background/Literature Review

This section contains a critical review of the literature concerning your area of study. Of note, this section must clearly relate to the research problem (outlined above). Further, references cited in this section must be in a scholarly format (e.g., APA style), and be included in a references section at the end of the thesis proposal. Here are some ways to structure a literature review.

Chronologically. This is perhaps the simplest approach, but it is not simply a listing of sources or citations in order. You will need to try to analyze any patterns that have emerged over time, and identify the key debates or turning points that may have shaped the direction of the field, and you would need to include some thoughts as to why these developments might have occurred.

Thematically. This structure will use a series of recurring themes to build the literature review. These can be the themes that you have identified in your conceptual model and have built your research questions on. For example, if you are looking at a topic such as the value of English in a particular country, then you may want to focus on social, economic, and educational aspects.

Methodologically. If you are looking at different disciplines that utilize a variety of research methods, then you might align the literature review with a discussion of each approach to research. You would then need to examine and present the research and conclusions that emerge from the different approaches (e.g., qualitative versus quantitative versus mixed-methods research; and empirical versus theoretical).

Theoretically. If the thesis is intended to discuss a theoretical framework or concept, then you can use it to present various theories, models, and definitions of key concepts. You might use it to argue the relevance of a specific theoretical approach to a practical problem, or combine a number of various theoretical concepts into a coherent argument for the development of a framework to support your research.

No matter the structure, the literature review should aim to compare and critique those studies that are the most relevant to the research problem(s) you are investigating. It is an extremely important part of a thesis proposal because it demonstrates that you have read the research available in your field of study and have utilized this research to be informed of the best way of attempting to resolve your research questions.

The literature review confirms that you have thoroughly searched the literature and understood what it means for your study. It proves that you have been able to distinguish good research from bad, as well as relevant research from irrelevant research. It must also provide what the literature supports as important in regards to your research problem or questions. In a literature review, you need to:

- give some background regarding the research problem;
- analyze what the literature says about the problem;
- define the meaning of important terms;
- explain how the research literature helps you to understand the problem under investigation; and
- provide any theoretical, conceptual or methodological framework that can help explain your problem.

Your advisor will point out if you have been able to provide the above to a sufficient standard.

The layout of your literature review may resemble the following:

Overview/Introduction. Explains how the review is organized.

Topic Headings. Organizes a critical review into topics associated with the research problem and questions. This might be based on the themes of your research questions or be organized using the following: key concepts, theories, and studies; key debates and controversies; or gaps in the literature.

Summary. Draw all of the main points together and describe what the review means for your thesis.

Research/Methods and Design

The methods section includes a statement as to the way(s) that you intend to investigate your thesis questions; design will indicate the steps for the methods process and provide further details. In other words, this is where you should explain your approach to the research and describe exactly what steps you took to answer your research questions.

This section is important because it shows that you have thought carefully about how you will carry out the research. That said, the structure and content of the research methods and design section of this document will depend on the nature of the research problem. There should be sufficient detail to enable your advisor to judge whether the study is likely to be successful or if some adjustments are required.

A further purpose of this section is to explain how and where you will carry out the data collection, and analysis. This will then determine the kind of ethics clearance that you may need before you can begin with data collection.

You need to give reasons as to why you have chosen a particular sample and method of data collection. You must also provide details concerning the data collection methods, including why and how those methods will be used and the site(s) where the data collection will occur. In this section you must:

- briefly outline your research method;
- state where your research will be carried out;
- describe what sample will be used, or who the participants will probably be;
- indicate the limitations that you perceive may arise when interpreting the results of the study;
- outline the steps that will be taken to overcome/minimize each limitation; and
- highlight any ethical implications or considerations that were taken into account.

Consider answering the following questions when writing this section:

- What kind of research design will be used? What are the advantages and limitations of that research design?
- What is the target population? Who will be my research participants? What and where are the research site/s?
- Will a sample be used? If so, how big will it be, how will it be selected, and will it be representative of the population?
- What instruments will be used? Do they include the researcher? How will they be selected/developed? What evidence will be given regarding their validity and reliability (or other standards)? Are they the best instruments to use?

- When will the data be collected or generated (in terms of time and relation to the research variables)? By whom?
- Will a pre-test or pilot study be used? If so, why? What action will be taken on the basis of the results?
- What methods of data analysis will be used? Why have these methods been chosen? Are they appropriate? Who will do the analysis?

An example layout might rely on the following sub-headings.

Research Design. Explain how you will design the research. Will it be qualitative or quantitative, or a mixed-method study? Will it rely on original data collection or primary and secondary sources? Will it be a descriptive, correlational, or experimental investigation?

Methods, Contexts and Sources. Describe the procedures, participants, instruments/tools, and sources of the research. When, where, and how will you collect, select, and analyze the data? Also take into account aspects of reliability and validity in this section, and show how you have met these factors in terms of your instruments and data collection.

Limitations of the Research. Address any potential obstacles, limitations, or other hindrances to the research in this section. How will you plan for these and work around them if necessary? If you are unable to generalize your results for any reason (e.g., use of a small sample of convenience), then explain that in this section, and state why your conclusions and research are still valid.

Ethical Issues. Depending on the nature of your research, you will need to consider ethical issues and implications concerning research development, and the way in which you will conduct your research. Regarding ethics, researchers have the following responsibilities.

- *Provide Information* - make the research aims clear to participants, and inform them of how the results will be used, and provide feedback to participants (including an opportunity for participants to verify the data collected about them).
- *Obtain Permission* - Written permission may be required. This may be in the form of an ethics clearance from the university, and/or from participants showing willingness to participate or from a child's guardian; from principles (to carry out research at a school); or, from teachers (allowing

you to sit in on classes and observe students). Participants should also be made aware that they have the right to withdraw from the study at any time.

- *Privacy/Confidentiality* – Provide a written guarantee of privacy and confidentiality to individuals and organizations from whom you collect data. Further, participants have the right to remain anonymous and you must change names so that participants cannot be identified.
- *Consideration* - Plan data collection so that there is as little disruption as possible for participants e.g., no lengthy absences from class, or any considerable interruption of lessons. Cooperate with people where you conduct the research (e.g., determine ahead of time if you will sit to observe classes, how and for what length of time you will record data, how you will be introduced, and so on).
- *Acknowledgements* - The cooperation and contribution of all participants should be acknowledged in a way that retains confidentiality unless otherwise requested.

Resources Required

Outline any special needs such as equipment or resources that is required to complete your thesis research, and if you have access to the required equipment or if you will need to secure it (e.g., particular software applications or recording hardware).

Data Storage

Ensure that you have a plan that sees you always maintaining a backup of data, both paper-based (such as original surveys) and electronic (such as a data repository). If you do not have a USB memory stick, you should obtain one and make regular backups of your thesis research on it. You could also use a cloud service such as Google Drive while conducting research as an interim storage solution or rely on more professional services like those of Figshare or Mendeley Data. You also need to be aware that the university where you study will have a policy regarding the length of time that you will need to keep all records regarding your thesis. This is so that your original data can be analyzed by a third party if required, and it is typically understood that you will keep these records for five to seven years.

Thesis Outline/Contents

Although different kinds of theses require different layouts, developing a guide to follow early on is important as it will help you maintain a research focus. The following is a common outline that you may include and develop with subheadings of your own:

- Abstract – 300 words.
- Definition of Terms – as required.
- Introduction – 3 to 5 pages.
- Literature Review – 15 to 20 pages.
- Research Methods and Design – 5 to 10 pages.
- Discussion and Results – 10 to 20 pages.
- Conclusion – 3 to 5 pages.
- References – in APA style.
- Appendices – as required.
- Glossary – as required.

Theoretical, Conceptual or Methodological Model/Framework

You may consider providing a graphical representation of how you intend to approach answering the research questions. Think of it as a blueprint, or the outline of how you plan to conduct the research for your thesis that also shows how your research sits/aligns within the larger field or scope of research. It is used to illustrate what you expect to find throughout your research, particularly how the variables that you are considering relate to each other.

There are many ways to go about creating a conceptual model. You may start with the main theme of your research broken down into three smaller themes (your research questions), with these then broken down into smaller concepts that you might then use to create survey or interview questions. These smaller concepts could all then be broken down further in order to develop interview questions from the survey, or follow-up questions from the main interview questions. The conceptual model or theoretical framework may simply show how all the variables of a study interrelate, e.g., what are the independent and the dependent variables and how they relate to each other and to the source of data or the context of the study. A graphical representation is an easy way for readers to see how things in your thesis relate to each other and how you will have undertaken the research.

Thesis Completion Schedule

Remember, you are not the only thesis student that your advisor works with, and in reality, a well-planned thesis and well-researched work should see you only need to meet with your advisor around four times if work is commented upon electronically and regularly. Keep in mind also that, without a schedule that you can commit to, you will not complete your thesis in the time allotted. Be realistic; don't think that you will complete your thesis in three weeks! By the time that you start your actual thesis research course, you will need to have a document like this one well and truly complete, and have already started to undertake research. You will likely have been engaging with participants (if there are any in your study), have had the method section complete, be reading to finalize the findings and conclusions, and be preparing for the oral defense.

You must remain constantly aware of the deadlines for submission of necessary documents, for example: the thesis defense period, the submission of first drafts to oral defense committee members, and so on. This information can usually be obtained from your graduate program handbook, from your department office assistants, and your thesis advisor.

References

Every reference that you cite must be included in a list of references at the end of your proposal, but do not include any reference which was not explicitly cited in your proposal. Ensure that the reference list adheres to the scholarly format decided upon by your graduate program, such as that of the American Psychological Association (APA).

Appendix (as required)

Add any additional items of importance in an appendix. At the thesis proposal stage, this might involve computer code, screen shots, or a listing of potential software that you need to narrow down for use in an experiment. It might also include samples of thematic coding and transcripts of audio interviews, and so on. A completed ethics proposal form could be placed here.

Glossary (as required)

If your thesis proposal contains a large number of specific or unique terms and/or a number of acronyms, it will be important to detail them all in a glossary section. List all the acronyms, terms, and key phrases in alphabetical order.

Common Problems

Some common problems found in the summary of the proposed research program could include:

- The abstract is not clear and precise, or it lacks information that an abstract should contain.
- The research problem/questions/objectives are missing or not defined at all.
- The background section is not clearly tied to the research problem.
- The significance of the study is confused with the background, or the significance section fails to define the significance clearly.
- The research method is poorly explained, or it does not clearly address the research problem or identify the questions.
- The research method is not feasible in the time or scope that the student has to be able to complete the thesis.
- The explanation or treatment of ethical issues is not raised or it is inadequate.

Remember!

This proposal, or more correctly the information within it, will ultimately become your thesis. Your advisor can assist in checking all parts of the proposal, but it is not their job to write the proposal for you or to sit with you while you come up with ideas to complete the thesis proposal. You must complete as much of this document as you possibly can *before* meeting your advisor.

Blank Thesis Proposal Template

Title of the Thesis

Thesis Advisor: Name

Semester, Year

Graduate Program Name
University Name

Your Name
Your Student Number

Abstract

Definition of Terms

If relevant, or placed into a glossary if not incorporated into the introduction or literature review.

Introduction

Background and context

Research Problem

Significance

Practical Implications

Theoretical Implications

Research Questions

1.

2.

3.

Literature Review

Overview/Introduction.

Headings

These should be research question-based, or those such as: key concepts, theories, and studies; key debates and controversies; and gaps in the literature.

Summary

Methodology and Design

Research Design

Methods and Sources

Procedure

Participants

Instruments

Context/Source

Practical Considerations

Limitations of the Research

Ethical Considerations

Other Considerations

Resources Required

Data Storage

Thesis Outline

Conceptual Model/Methodological Framework

Thesis Completion Schedule

Research Phase	Objectives	Deadline

References

Appendices

Glossary

Human Research Ethics Application

TESOL Graduate Program
Human Research Ethics Application (HREA)
ETHICS REVIEW FORM

Office Use Only	Received:	
	Advisor:	
	Ethics Review No:	

Purpose

The HREA was developed in order to assist researchers in considering the ethical principles of the Guideline for Establishment of Research Ethics (Instruction of the Korean Ministry of Education No. 153) in relation to their research.

Level of Ethical Review

Indicate the level of ethical review that is being sought for this application.

☐ **Full HREA Review**
Applies to all research involving more than 'low risk research'.

☐ **Low Risk Review**
Applies to 'low risk research' which is research that can generally be undertaken by an individual (e.g., involves one-site research: research across a single classroom or several of the researchers' classrooms, and conducted in a single country).

Section 1: Project and Researcher's Details

1.1. Project focus/objective (e.g., classroom observational process, developing vocabulary skills with *app name*, etc.)

1.2. Project timeframe (tick those that apply):

- ☐ Spring semester ☐ Summer session
- ☐ Fall semester ☐ Winter session

Other (______________________________)

1.3. Main researcher

Name ____________________ ID: __________

Research Role ______________________________

1.4. Others, such as research assistants, secondary investigators If the research involves use of assistants, requires volunteers, or the participation of other teachers, please list them here.

Name ____________________ ID: __________

Research Role ______________________________

Name ____________________ ID: __________

Research Role ______________________________

Name ____________________ ID: __________

Research Role ______________________________

Section 2: Nature of the Project

2.1. Rationale of the project (e.g., why are you undertaking the research? Filling gaps in literature, contribute new knowledge to field, research for CPD, research for a conference presentation.)

2.2. Research interaction (e.g., describe the interactions between researchers and participants, such as teacher-student, or not involved as looking at data sets collected by third parties like administration.)

2.3. Location(s) of the research (Include details of all sites and times where the project will be undertaken and locations of participants, e.g., classroom, in-office interviews, over six weeks during class/homework, conducted mid-semester three weeks prior to midterm and three weeks post-midterm.)

2.4. If the research is to be conducted with or about participants living outside Korea, outline any local legislation, regulations, permissions, or customs that need to be addressed before the research can commence. Outline the steps taken to ensure that this has been adequately considered and addressed.

Section 3: Participants and Recruitment

3.1. Who will be the participants in this project? (e.g., administration, teachers only, students only, students and teachers, a single GCT reading class.)

3.2. How does the research comply with participant consent? (e.g., permission granted by participants to record their images or voice for research purposes, right to decline participation has been granted.)

3.3. What steps are being used to protect the anonymity of participants and the research data collected? (e.g., coding the data, obtaining pre-coded data, use of anonymous surveys.)

3.4. Will you obtain/do you have consent to use the collected data for research purposes? (e.g., a participation sheet has been provided to appropriate participants or those providing research data.)

3.5. What materials will be used to recruit participants and how will they be used? Provide details of any posters, flyers, participant information sheets, consent forms, advertisements, emails, and letters that will be used. Include a listing of any online or physical sites or advertisements that have been or will be used to collect the data. (e.g., a Google Forms account has been used to record student/teacher survey responses.)

3.6. How and by whom will initial contact between the researcher and participants be made? (e.g., teacher will ask in class, teacher will ask administration, administration will ask the teacher/students, teacher will recruit on Facebook/at a conference.)

3.7. Describe how, when, and what information about the proposed research activities will be provided to participants and any third parties. (e.g., participants can publicly review the lead researcher profile on Research Gate and obtain the completed research product from such a site, research is made available to all faculty/students by the department website or university official blogs, research conducted and presented at a conference is made publicly available by sharing the notes/ppt as appropriate.)

3.8. For participants who are not fluent in English or who have difficulty understanding English, what arrangements will be made to ensure comprehension of the research information if any? (e.g., translation of surveys into native language.)

3.9. What research activities have been, or will be, conducted during the process of data gathering?

Research method/activity		**Participant time**	**Research method/Activity**		**Participant time**
Action research	☐		Interview	☐	
Data linkage	☐		Observation	☐	
Ethnographic	☐		Survey	☐	
Focus group	☐		Textual analysis	☐	
Intervention	☐		Use of data sets	☐	

Other (________________________________)

Section 4 Ethical Considerations

In addition to the ethical considerations pertaining to all research participants, researchers should be aware of the specific issues that arise in terms of the design, conduct, and ethical review of research involving various categories of participants as outlined in the *National Statement Section 4.*

4.1. Do you foresee any burdens or risks to participants or researchers? (Burdens include impact on participants such as inconvenience, e.g., those that are minor such as filling in a form, giving up time to participate in research, or those that are major such as anxiety induced by interview. Other risks may be emotional, social, legal, medical, or physical, and can include distress and harm.)

____

____

____

____

____

____

____

____

____

____

____

____

____

4.2. Describe how the burdens/risks will be minimized or mitigated as necessary.

4.3. Describe how researcher(s) will protect the privacy and confidentiality of participants (e.g., anonymous encoding of research data.)

4.4. Will any inducement for participation be made available, who will provide it, and how will it be provided? (e.g., Starbucks coffee vouchers delivered by SMS paid for with a research grant; participation points provided to students to increase their grades.)

Section 5: Data Confidentiality, Analysis, Reporting, Storage, and Future Use

5.1. Select the option that reflects the type of data that will be accessed throughout the research.

Note. For some research, the type of data received or collected may initially be different to the type of data that is stored. For example, interview data with names recorded is individually identifiable data. If names are *permanently* removed when the data is stored at the completion of the project, the data would be considered non-identifiable. Personally identifiable information is any detail that can be used to identify a particular individual. This may include name, email, phone number, student/employee ID, position, or rank.

Type of Data	Initially Received/ Collected	Stored (at completion)
Non-identifiable: participant data that is received or collected in a non-identifiable form, including data which has never had personal identifiers, e.g., an anonymous survey or a survey from which identifiers have been permanently removed before the researcher(s) receive it. It is not possible for the researcher(s) to identify specific individuals.	☐	☐
Re-identifiable: participant data from which personal identifiers have been removed and replaced by code(s). The data is either received with codes already attached with the personal identifiers removed or the researcher(s) remove the identifiers and replace them with code(s). It remains possible for at least one researcher to re-identify a specific individual by, for example, using the code(s) or linking to a different data set or to different data sets.	☐	☐
Individually Identifiable: participant data where an individual's identity can be reasonably ascertained via a (nick)name, student number, position in an organization, and so on.	☐	☐

5.2. How will the privacy and confidentiality of participant data, samples, and information be protected during the collection and/or recruitment phase? (Outline the de-identification processes, separation of roles of those responsible for the management of data, and any other relevant practices. Outline where data will be stored during the data collection phase and who will have access to it.)

5.3. How will the privacy and confidentiality of participant data, samples, and information be protected during the data analysis and write-up phases? (Outline the de-identification processes, use of pseudonyms, codes, or explicit consent, and any other relevant practices.)

5.4. How will participant data, samples, and information be analyzed and who will undertake this analysis? (e.g., t-test using SPSS conducted by the second researcher.)

5.5. What feedback of findings will be offered to participants? (e.g., access to transcripts of interviews, drafts, or final reports when they become available. If no feedback is to be offered, outline why. Note that it may be good practice to conduct member checking of any collected data.)

5.6. How will the project outcomes be made publicly accessible at the end of the project and in what forms (e.g., journal article, book, conference paper, in the media, presentation, stored in a library). If they will not be made publicly accessible, detail how the research will be applied (e.g., presented to a committee).

5.7. Outline how the records, materials, and data from the project will be stored on completion and for how long, or if they will be destroyed. Include details of the storage location and who will have access. (Note that the minimum period for retention of research data is five years from the date of any publication, and that this varies depending on the specific type of research.)

5.8. Who will be the data custodian? (All data collections should have an identified custodian to enable access by researchers or participants to the data while maintaining it in a protected form. The custodian of the data may be the individual researcher, the agency that collected the information, or an intermediary who manages data coming from a number of sources.)

5.9. For future use of data and/or its re-issue, what type of consent will be obtained? Will consent be specific, extended, or unspecified? (Data collected as part of a research project can only be shared or used in future with the explicit consent of the participants. Ideally, if the data is collected and stored in such a way that it can be used in future research projects then the participant information sheet and consent forms should outline this and make that clear to participants.)

5.10. If specific consent is sought, justify why the data and information generated by this research should not be made available for future research. (e.g., Where a researcher believes that there are ethical reasons not to make research data or information accessible for future use, this must be justified.)

5.11. Data custody: maintain the data from the project as data custodian. (If future use or sharing of the data is intended, participants are to be fully informed of this in the participant information sheet, in the survey that they complete, or during interview recording. Data custodianship will be the responsibility of the researcher.)

Section 6: Conflict of Interest or Other Ethical Issues

6.1. Outline the source of any project funding.

____

____

____

____

____

____

6.2. Outline any 'conflict of interest' issues that may arise during the project.

____

____

____

____

____

____

6.3. Do the researchers expect to obtain any direct or indirect financial or other benefits through conducting this research?

____

____

____

____

____

6.4. Outline any other ethical or relevant issues not discussed on this form.

____

____

____

____

____

____

Section 7: Declaration by the Researcher(s)

I/we have read the *Guideline for Establishment of Research Ethics (Instruction of the Korean Ministry of Education No. 153).*

I/we the researcher(s) agree to:

- conduct the project in accordance with our responsibilities under the Korean Ministry of Education and University guidelines;
- begin collecting data only after submission of the human research ethics application has been reviewed;
- only carry out this research project where adequate funding and personnel is available to enable the project to be carried out according to good research practice and in an ethical manner;
- notify the ethics committee in writing in the event of any adverse or unforeseen events occurring prior, during, or after the commencement of research, at the discontinuation of research, and changes to those involved in the research; and
- participate in an audit if requested by the ethics committee.

In addition, as researcher/applicant, I/we:

- accept responsibility for the conduct of this research project in accordance with the *Guideline for Establishment of Research Ethics (Instruction of the Korean Ministry of Education No. 153)*;
- certify that all researchers and other personnel involved in this project are appropriately qualified and experienced or will undergo appropriate training and supervision to fulfil their role in this project; and
- will take responsibility for the confidential maintenance of the research materials as per the *Guideline for Establishment of Research Ethics (Instruction of the Korean Ministry of Education No. 153)* and as required by legislation.

All persons named in **Section 1** are required to sign below:

Researcher's Signature: ______________________________

Name: ______________________________ Date: ____________

Assistant's Signature: ______________________________

Name: ______________________________ Date: ____________

Assistant's Signature: ______________________________

Name: ______________________________ Date: ____________

Assistant's Signature: ______________________________

Name: ______________________________ Date: ____________

Section 8: Checklist

The following documents (if appropriate) are attached to the main body of the application, and are clearly labeled using the appropriate number (i.e., Attachment 1, Attachment 2, etc.). Check Y for Yes, N for No, or N/A for not applicable.

Y	N	N/A	Item	Attachment
☐	☐	☐	Participant information including contacts for complaints either as an information sheet, verbal script, or survey preamble.	
☐	☐	☐	The standard consent form for a participant in a research project. (Written consent is required for the majority of projects.)	
☐	☐	☐	Consent by a third party to complete the participation form. (This is required where participants are under 18 years or a dependent adult.)	
☐	☐	☐	Other recruitment documentation including advertisements, flyers, recruitment letters, emails of introduction, copy of Facebook event pages, and social media event sites.	
☐	☐	☐	Procedure/protocol for interviews or focus groups including topics, questions, and themes.	
☐	☐	☐	Survey instrument/questionnaire. (Include a printed copy of the survey.)	
☐	☐	☐	Evidence of approval/rejection by other human research ethics committees, including comments and requested alterations to the application, if applicable.	
☐	☐	☐	Research with people outside Korea: evidence of permissions, approvals from overseas authorities, and so on.	

Section 9: How to Submit this Application

1. Print the completed form and obtain signatures from all researchers.

2. Scan the signed form including all labeled attachments as **one pdf file** and email it to the chair of the ethics committee.

3. Submission deadlines:
   Full HREA review: end of the semester prior to research commencement.
   Low risk HREA review: submit at any time.
   Allow for the possibility that a project submitted as a low-risk application may be deemed to involve more than low risk, or to raise other issues, which would therefore require a full committee review.

4. Be aware that in all cases, researchers may be requested to provide additional information, as well as a copy of their research results (e.g., journal article, presentation notes/ppt, thesis).

Note. References to the *Guideline for the Establishment of Research Ethics* throughout this form are not meant to be exhaustive but rather to provide a starting point for researchers to consider. Researchers should be familiar with these guidelines when conducting research from within Korea and during their time at the university.

Sample Participant Consent Form

Participant Name: ______________________________

Research Project Title:

____

Research Description:

____

____

____

____

- I have read the research description and have had the opportunity to ask questions about the purposes and procedures regarding this study.
- My participation in this research is voluntary. I may refuse to participate or withdraw from participation at any time without retribution.
- The researcher may withdraw me from the research at their professional discretion.
- Any information derived from the research project that personally identifies me will not be released or disclosed without my separate consent, except as specifically required by law.
- If at any time I have any questions regarding the research or my participation, I can contact the researcher by email at ______________________.
- If at any time I have comments or concerns regarding the conduct of the research or questions about my rights as a research subject, I should contact the advisor Dr. ______________ by email at ______________________.
- I give my consent to be audio-recorded and/or video-recorded and/or for any written or electronic material that I have completed to be used for research purposes.
- My signature, or electronic statement, means that I agree to participate in this study.

Participant's signature: ________________ Date: __________

Photocopiable Content – Thesis

Plagiarism Analysis Report				
Author Details	Name ____________			
	Student Number ____________			
	Department ____________			
	Major ____________			
	Graduate Program ____________			
Degree	☐ Master's ☐ Doctorate			
Course[1]	Name of course ____________			
Title[2]	____________ ____________			
Plagiarism	☐ 0-9% Secure	☐ 10-15% Caution	☐ 16-20% Suspicious	☐ >20% Risk
Comments[3]	____________ ____________ ____________ ____________ ____________			
Attachments[4]	☐ Plagiarism report ☐ Other			
Student Signature ____________				
Professor/Advisor Signature ____________				
Date ____________				

1. Complete if appropriate.
2. Assignment, thesis, or dissertation title.
3. Comments to be made by the course professor/thesis advisor in terms of recommendations for the student (if any).
4. Attach the plagiarism report provided by the application recommended by your school, and any other necessary documents as advised.

Thesis Cheat Sheet

Abstract

Background. Provide a link to the thesis purpose/problem.

Methodology. Include participant information, instruments, context, and design.

Results. Basic findings, conclusions, recommendations.

Final remarks. Additional findings of importance, real-world implications, limitations and future research possibilities.

Introduction

Introduce the topic. State the problem or area of focus with background information.

Significance. Explain why the research is valuable/important. Provide a statement of significance: *The research will be of value to/for …*

Purpose of the study. Describe the purpose for undertaking the research. *The purpose of this thesis is to examine … The specific research questions are …*

Literature Review

Develop this section in order to support the process and purpose of your study – use peer-reviewed journal articles.

Breakdown the literature review into important sub-topics relevant to your investigation using headings and sub-headings.

Aim to explore the key concepts, theories, and studies.

Identify the key debates and controversies, and any gaps in existing knowledge.

Methodology

Rationale. Detail the methods and state why they best fit the research design, and the rationale for using those particular methods instead of others. The methodological framework or the conceptual model can be presented here.

Participant data. Information on those who form part of the study.

Instrument information. Detail the development and type used to collect the data, including any reliability and validity.

Context. Situate the study, and discuss and detail the context (e.g., school, environment of the study, and so on).

Findings

Restate the research questions. You could do this using the theme of each question as a heading or the major themes that emerge from findings.

Describe the data that answers the questions.

Present emerging themes, categories, and patterns in the data.

Detail the findings with tables, graphs, figures, and so on as required.

Summarize the results with foundational interpretations of what the findings indicate.

Conclusions

Overview. State what the chapter will cover.

Conclusions. Present these based on the findings.

Impact of the study in terms of what was learned, supported by the strengths of the study then follows.

Limitations of the study, including any problems you had, as well as what the results may not be able to tell us are then covered.

Implications for the field (practical ones), for theory, and for future studies are then highlighted.

Recommendations for further research, changes in academic concepts, knowledge or professional practice, modifications of accepted theoretical constructs, or changes in organizations, procedures and practice, behavior, policies, and so on are then presented.

Summary. Finally, provide a short summary of the answers to the research questions and ultimately what your thesis has achieved.

References

All works cited in the thesis must be listed using an accepted scholarly citation method (e.g., APA style).

Appendices

Include all supporting evidence that was not presented in the main body of the thesis here (e.g., instruments, transcripts of interviews, coding of interviews, software code, and so on).

Glossary

List all acronyms, provide definitions of terms or key words.

Basic Referencing
(APA Style 7th Edition)

In-Text Citations

A work with one or two authors
… Author and Author (Year) found that …
… (Author & Author, Year).

A Work by Three or More Authors
Author et al. (Year) argued that …
… (Author et al., Year).

Two or More Works in the Same Parenthesis
… (Author, Year; Author, Year).

In References

Periodicals
Author, A. A. (Year). Title of article. *Title of Periodical, volume number*(issue number), pages. DOI
Author, A. A., & Author, B. B. (Year). Title of article. *Title of Periodical, volume number*(issue number), pages. DOI

Proceedings
Author, A. A., & Author, B. B. (Eds.). (Year). *Title of Proceedings.* Publisher. URL

Presentations
Contributor, A. A., & Contributor, B. B. (Year, Month Day). *Title of contribution* [Description of contribution e.g., Keynote]. Title of Symposium/Conference, Location. URL

Book
Author, A. A. (Year). *Title of book: Capital letter also for subtitle.* Publisher Name.

Book in Another Language

Author, A. A. (Year). *Title of Book [Translation of book title]. Publisher.]*

Edited Book

Editor, E. E. (Ed.). (Year). *Title of book: Capital letter also for subtitle.* Publisher.

Chapter in an Edited Book

Author, A. A. (Year). Title of chapter. In E. E. Editor (Ed.), *Title of book*, (pp. #-#). Publisher Name.

Unpublished Dissertation and Theses

Author, A. A. (Year). *Title of dissertation* [Unpublished doctoral dissertation]. Name of Institution Awarding the Degree.

Author, A. A. (Year). *Title of thesis* [Unpublished master's thesis]. Name of Institution Awarding the Degree.

Website

Author, A. A. (Date). *Title of page*. Site Name. URL

YouTube Video

Uploader, A. A. (Date). Title of work [Description]. YouTube. URL

Note. There are a number of other basic rules to follow when using APA style. These include ways to format a reference list, how to format a paper, and how to accurately cite a range of other print and non-print sources.

Glossary

Academic advisor	An academic advisor typically works with college and university students in a counseling role. They are available to help students if they experience any issues or problems with their classes, and to help them if they need it in regard to taking a portfolio or thesis completion track. They are also responsible for ensuring that the student is fulfilling degree completion requirements in a timely manner.
Advisor	The advisor role is to provide guidance, and to ensure that the tasks that need to be performed are understood. They will at times also be responsible for evaluating your performance.
APA	American Psychological Association
CELT	An extensive integrative educational task undertaken as a final project in an academic/degree program (e.g., practicum, portfolio, thesis).
Citation	Culture and English language teaching.
Clinical observation	The process of being observed by a colleague or peer that can be trusted so that they can offer mentorship, feedback, and guidance on your teaching performance.
CLT	*See* **communicative language teaching**.
Communicative language teaching	In this approach to language teaching, there is an emphasis on the four skills (listening, speaking, reading, and writing) with more of a focus on communicative competence than linguistic competence. It is often referred to as **CLT.**
Copyright	An exclusive legal right that is given to an originator of a work, or an assignee, to print, publish, perform, film or record literary,

articstic, or musical material, and to authorize others to do so as well.

Defense committee This is a panel of experts that may convene at an oral defense for a college or university student's thesis completion requirements. It will typically consist of a minimum of a committee chair, the student's thesis advisor, and another examiner.

Ethical issues Ethical issues and their consideration, particularly for educators and researchers, are those of privacy, respecting the anonymity and confidentiality of participants and their data, a need to acquire informed consent, and a need to ensure involve beneficence.

KATE The Korea Association for Teachers of English.

KCI The **Korean Citation Index** is a listing of those peer-reviewed journals who are indexed at this scholarly level. It is often considered to be easier to publish at this level as opposed to that of **Scopus** or **SCI**. There are also other indexes such as SSCI. This allows academic researchers to identify the quality of articles being read, and the demands and rigors that were placed on the researcher during the publication process.

KOTESOL The Korean Organization of Teachers to Speakers of Other Languages.

MALL Multimedia assisted language learning.

Mixed-methods This kind of research is an approach whereby an investigator will collect and analyze both quantitative and qualitative data within the same study.

Oral defense An oral defense or **viva** is an oral examination in which a college or university student defends their thesis in front of a panel of experts (the

	defense committee) as part of the process for fulfilling the requirements to obtain their degree.
Peer observation	Observing a colleague teach. Peer observation provides both the observer and the observee with the opportunity to mutually enhance the quality of their teaching practice.
Personal learning network	A **personal learning network (PLN)** refers to the combination of tools, people, and services that an individual utilizes as resources and approaches to learning (both personally for enrichment and for professional development purposes).
PLN	*See* **Personal learning network (PLN)**.
Portfolio	The portfolio is typically undertaken by those college or university students who do not wish to complete a thesis. It serves as a means for prospective and in-service teachers to showcase their learning, consider their competency as a classroom teacher, and engage in the reflection of their learning and of the coursework that they have competed while undertaking graduate study.
PPP	*See* **Presentation, practice, production**.
Practicum	A practicum is a process that a student/practicing teacher will undertake in order to develop and practice the craft of teaching. It provides them with a means to put into practice what they have learned in theory. The goal is to have practicing teachers partner with supervising teachers. The practicum experience typically involves a combination of self-observation, peer observation, and clinical supervision.
Practicing teacher	A practicing, or practice teacher, also known as a student teacher, is a college, university, or

graduate student who is teaching under the supervision of a supervisory teacher in order to qualify for a degree.

Presentation, practice, production A communicative teaching technique that involves the teacher presenting language points, the teacher and students practicing together, and then the students producing the language points learned on their own. *Also known as* **PPP.**

Qualitative This kind of research is a method of scientific inquiry that relies upon non-numerical data, placing the focus on meaning-making. Examples might include diary accounts, ethnography, interview, as well as participant observation.

Quantifiers Words that are used to indicate how much, or how many, of a thing we are referring to, e.g., a lot of, many.

Quantitative This kind of research is a method of scientific inquiry that relies upon empirical investigation via computational, mathematical, or statistical techniques. Examples can include test data analysis.

Reliability A reliable item, test, and whatever else, is one that provides consistent means of producing an outcome (e.g., it can be marked the same way by all people tasked to mark the test).

SCI *See* **science citation index**.

Science citation index The **science citation index** is a listing of those peer-reviewed journal articles that are indexed at this scholarly level. It is often abbreviated to the acronym **SCI**. There are also other indexes such as SSCI, **Scopus**, and **KCI**. This allows academic researchers to identify the quality of articles being read, and the demands and rigors

	that were placed on the researcher during the publication process.
Scopus	A listing of those peer-reviewed journal articles that are indexed at this scholarly level. It is often considered to be easier to publish at this level as opposed to that of **SCI**. There are also other indexes such as SSCI, and **KCI**. This allows academic researchers to identify the quality of articles being read, and the demands and rigors that were placed on the researcher during the publication process.
Self-observation	Observing yourself, or your performance as a teacher, can help you be reflective in terms of evaluating if what you are doing as a teacher is successful.
SIG	A **special interest group** is a community, online or offline, within a larger organization that consists of members who hold a particular interest in advancing a specific area of knowledge, learning or technology.
Special interest group	A **SIG** refers to a community, online or offline, within a larger organization that consists of members who hold a particular interest in advancing a specific area of knowledge, learning or technology.
STEM	The Society of Teaching English through Media.
Student talk time	This is the time that a student spends talking during a lesson, and it can be compared to **teacher-talk-time (TTT).**
Student teacher	A student teacher, practicing, or practice teacher is a college, university or graduate student who is teaching under the supervision of a supervisory teacher in order to qualify for a degree.

ST(T)	*See* **student-talk (time).**
Supervisory teacher	A teacher who provides you with mentorship, feedback, observation, and guidance during peer and clinical observations, typically as part of a practicum experience.
Teacher talk time	The time that a teacher spends talking during a lesson, and it can be compared to **student-talk-time (STT)**.
TESOL	Teaching English to speakers of other languages.
Thesis	A long, structured essay involving personal research that is written by a candidate for a college or university degree, typically a master's degree with a dissertation written for a doctoral degree.
Thesis advisor	This is the person who supervises the progress of a college or university student who is undertaking thesis research.
Thesis proposal	A thesis proposal is a document that a college or university student prepares which outlines their proposed thesis topic. It typically defines the research agenda and topic under investigation, detailing why the topic warrants research and how the student will undertake it.
Total physical response	A method of language teaching utilizing physical (motor) activity during lessons. *See* **TPR**.
TPR	*See* **total physical response**.
TTT	*See* **teacher talk time (TTT)**.
Validity	A valid item, test, and whatever else, is one that does what it says that it will do.
Viva	*See* **Oral defense**.
Work product	A work product, in terms of a portfolio item, might include any material that a college or

university student has developed during their course of study, and can range from a conference, class, symposium, or workshop presentation using PowerPoint, a literature review, an annotated bibliography, a research project, or a pedagogy project/lesson plan.

Useful Resources

As sites continuously go down, merge, and emerge, perhaps only a small selection of all appropriate resource content should be presented here. An attempt at keeping the number of resources to a select few for each type also provides a sample that is both comprehensive and extensive, but not overwhelming. Like any other instructor resource list, individuals will be able to add to the content as they find material that is useful, and over time, curate a vast resource library tailored to their individual teaching and learning context. Teachers who wish to record any additional resources that they come across might like to use the notes section that follows this chapter for that purpose.

The following content is covered:

- Associations
- Citations
- Data driven learning
- Data repositories
- Grammar
- Journals
- Lesson plans
- Online Short Course Providers
- Plagiarism
- Portfolio development
- Praxis tests
- Presentations
- Professional development resources
- Writing

Associations

ACTA (https://tesol.org.au) is the Australian Council for TESOL Associations.

ALTA (http://altaonweb.org) is the African Language Teachers Association.

AsiaTEFL (http://www.asiatefl.org) is the Asian Association of Teachers of English as a Foreign Language.

EUROCALL (http://www.eurocall-languages.org) is the European Association for Computer-Assisted Language Learning.

TESOL International (https://www.tesol.org) is the Teaching of English to Speakers of Other Languages Association that is based in the United States of America.

IATEFL (https://www.iatefl.org) is the International Association for the Teaching of English as a Foreign Language, and it is based in the United Kingdom.

JALT (https://jalt.org) is the Japanese Association of Language Teachers.

KOTESOL (https://koreatesol.org) is the Korea Association for the Teachers of English to Speakers of Other Languages.

SinoTESOL (http://www.sinotesol.com) is the Chinese Organization of Teachers of English to Speakers of Other Languages.

ThaiTESOL (https://www.thailandtesol.org) is the Thailand Association of Teachers of English to Speakers of Other Languages.

Citations

Cite this for me (https://www.citethisforme.com) is a citation tool that can help you to create a bibliography using the citation style of your choice.

EndNote (https://endnote.com) is a tool that is useful for managing and publishing bibliographies, citations, and references.

Refworks (https://www.refworks.com/refworks2) is a useful tool for managing and organizing bibliographies.

Mendeley (https://www.mendeley.com) is a good tool for reference management and for collaborating and sharing work.

Zotero (https://www.zotero.org) is a good tool for the management and organization of different resources and for the sharing of research.

Data Driven Learning

ANtWordProfiler (http://www.laurenceanthony.net/software/antwordprofiler) is a freeware tool that can be used to profile the vocabulary level and complexity level of texts. It can be downloaded for use on a Linux, MacOS, or Windows-based operating system.

Compleat Lexical Tutor (https://www.lextutor.ca) provides a range of tools that allow for the analysis of text so that you can develop data-driven learning content that can then be used with your students. Tools include vocabulary profiling, concordance, and so on.

English Corpora (https://www.english-corpora.org) provides links to widely-used online English language corpora.

Rewordify (https://rewordify.com) will reword any text that you provide into a simpler format that makes it easier for students to read. It identifies the language that it has reworded so that students and teachers know what has been changed. It also offers the ability to create quizzes from the content that you provide, including matching and cloze exercise types.

Word Families (https://www.enchantedlearning.com/rhymes/word families) is a useful resource that provides ready-to-print word wheels and word-family minibooks to use with learners.

Data Repositories

Figshare (https://figshare.com) is a free knowledge repository where users can make all research output available in a citable, shareable and discoverable manner.

Mendeley Data (https://data.mendeley.com) Allows researchers to upload their data, store it, share it with select users, make it publicly available and citable, as well as publish it.

Grammar

Grammar Girl's Quick and Dirty Tips for Better Writing (https://www.quickanddirtytips.com/grammar-girl) is run across various social media platforms including a YouTube channel, webpage, podcast, and Facebook page that all offer quick and dirty writing, vocabulary, and language tips.

Grammarly (https://app.grammarly.com) is a free writing app that analyses the text that you have written and provides feedback for clarity, and grammar. It also offers a plagiarism checking service for a fee.

Linguapress (https://linguapress.com) offers free grammar resources online and printable resources for teachers and students, including readings and games. There is also an area for teachers who need a grammar refresher to brush up on their skills.

Journals

Computer Assisted Language Learning Journal (https://www.tandfonline.com/loi/ncal20) is SCI indexed and published by Taylor & Francis.

Journal of Education and E-Learning research (https://www.asianonlinejournals.com/index.php/JEELR) is SCOPUS indexed and published by the Asian Online Journal Publishing Group (AOJPG).

Korean Citation Index (https://www.kci.go.kr/kciportal/main.kci) maintains a list of Korean peer-reviewed and KCI listed titles.

Language Learning and Technology (https://www.lltjournal. org) is SCI indexed, and published out of the University of Hawaii.

SCOPUS (https://www.scopus.com) maintains a list of peer-reviewed journal titles indexed in SCOPUS.

The Asian EFL Journal (https://www.asian-efl-journal.com) is SCI indexed and published by E.L.E.

The Journal of AsiaTEFL (http://journal.asiatefl.org/) is SCOPUS indexed and published by the Asian Association of Teachers of English as a Foreign Language.

The Journal of Teaching English with Technology (https://www.tewtjournal.org/) is SCOPUS indexed and published by the IATEFL Poland Computer Special Interest Group and the University of Nicosia.

The RELC Journal (https://journals.sagepub.com/home/rel) is SCOPUS indexed, and out of the Regional Language Center of the Southeast Asian Ministers of Education Organization.

TESOL Quarterly (https://onlinelibrary.wiley.com/journal/ 15457249) is SCI indexed and published by Wiley-Blackwell on behalf of the TESOL International Association.

Web of Science Master Journal List (https://mjl.clarivate.com/ home) maintains SCI indexed journals.

Lesson Plans

Breaking News English (https://breakingnewsenglish.com) offers a range of news articles broken down by levels, and it comes with a complete lesson plan for implementation.

Busy teacher (https://busyteacher.org) provides over 17,000 printable worksheets and lesson plans.

ESL Brains (https://eslbrains.com) publishes a variety of worksheets based around various videos, including those of TED talks. Lesson plans based on topic and level are also searchable.

Esllibrary.com (https://esllibrary.com) offers a range of lesson plans for EFL/ESL teachers to either use as is, or with some modification to suit their learners and teaching context.

ICALTEFL Lesson Plans & Activities (https://www.icaltefl.com/category/lesson-plans-activities) website offers a range of ideas, activities, and lesson plans that a teacher might choose to use with their learners.

One Stop English (http://www.onestopenglish.com) offers a range of materials for use with business and ESP classes for exams, for grammar, and a range of language skills, as well as for various ages. There is also a section on teacher resources and professional development.

Online Short Course Providers

Coursera (https://www.coursera.org) offers free courses in a variety of subject areas that are offered online from world-class universities and companies.

FutureLearn (https://www.futurelearn.com/) provides online study options from short courses through to postgraduate degrees across a wide variety of categories and from a wide variety of universities and organizations.

Study.com (https://study.com) is a site designed to deliver online courses for students, teachers, homeschool, college credit, and for test preparation.

Plagiarism

Copyscape (https://www.copyscape.com) is an online plagiarism checker that can be used to detect duplicate text on the internet.

Grammarly (https://app.grammarly.com) is a free writing app that analyzes the text that you have written and provides feedback for clarity and grammar. It also offers a plagiarism checking service for a fee.

Plagiarisma (http://plagiarisma.net) is a free online plagiarism checker for academics, students, and teachers.

Quetext (https://quetext.com) is an online citation generator and plagiarism checker. It will compare text to webpages, academic sources, news sources, and online textbooks.

Turnitin (https://turnitin.com) is one of the most widely used plagiarism checkers in academia, and it is often licensed by universities for faculty use.

Portfolio Development

Evernote (https://evernote.com) allows you to digitally organize a range of content, including notes and to-do lists, and to complete a range of task management activities and provide archiving for them all.

LiveBinders (http://livebinders.com) is an organization and eportfolio tool that allows you to integrate a variety of content into one location.

Seesaw: The Learning Journal (https://web.seesaw.me) is a versatile digital portfolio creation app that anyone can use to showcase their learning by uploading content and providing annotation.

VoiceThread (https://voicethread.com) allows users to import various media such as images, PowerPoints, and PDFs. It provides a means of making audio or video recordings concerning those media artifacts, and it also allows other users to reply to the initial comments by audio or video means.

Praxis Tests

Praxis Tests – ETS (https://www.ets.org/praxis) provides information on the test, and allows for registration to take the test.

Praxis ESL (https://study.com/academy/course/praxis-esl-practice-and-study-guide.html) is a short online course, which is free, and reviews the material found in the praxis test for teachers of English to speakers of other languages.

Presentations

Glogster (https://edu.glogster.com) allows students to create online multimedia posters, or Glogs, from a combination of media types from audio and graphic to video as well as hyperlinks.

Google Slides (https://www.google.com/slides/about) allows those with a Google account a means of creating, editing, and collaborating with others on presentations.

LinkedIn SlideShare (https://www.slideshare.net) allows users to search for presentations, infographics, documents, and other items on topics of their interest.

Microsoft PowerPoint Online (https://www.office.com/launch/powerpoint) extends the Microsoft PowerPoint experience to the web browser with OneDrive integration, and allows users to create, edit, and view files on the go.

Padlet (https://padlet.com) is a tool that allows learners to collaborate online by posting text, images, links, documents, videos, and voice recordings to their class page.

Prezi (https://prezi.com) is a visually-oriented presentation package that also allows users to upload PowerPoint slides and customize them, or use a variety of their own images, text, audio, and video.

Slidebean (https://slidebean.com) offers a one-click presentation development system that incorporates a variety of templates into the design of presentations.

VoiceThread (https://voicethread.com) allows users to import various media such as images, PowerPoints, and PDFs. It provides a means of making audio or video recordings concerning those media artifacts, and it also allows other users to reply to the initial comments, by audio or video means, as the presentation progresses.

Professional Development Resources

Developing Teachers (http://www.developingteachers.com/ index.htm) is a website that provides a range of resources for teachers, along with a variety of content that teachers can use to help make themselves better at their craft.

Ditchthattextbook (https://ditchthattextbook.com) is a website that offers various tips and insights into how to teach, and provides ways to use various technologies to assist in teaching.

Educational Technology and Mobile Learning (https://www.educatorstechnology.com) is a resource of educational web tools and mobile apps for teachers and educators.

Peachypublications (https://peachypublications.com) provides a range of books for teacher development along with a range of and lesson resources.

TEFLpedia (https://teflpedia.com) is a wiki that provides information on all aspects of teaching English as a foreign language.

TEFLVideos (http://www.teflvideos.com) is a dedicated professional development website for teachers of English to speakers of other languages that provides a range of content to help instructors improve upon their teaching.

Teaching English | British Council (https://www.teachingenglish.org.uk) offers a range of resources from their website, including those that focus on teacher development. The site also contains an ELT research database.

Writing

Purdue OWL (https://owl.purdue.edu/owl/purdue_owl.html) is the Purdue University Online Writing Lab. It provides access to a wide range of writing resources and instructional content. It provides access to the latest citation styles with examples that can help junior, and senior researchers, in following academic standards.

Notes

About the Book

Capstone Projects, the fourth in the Issues in TESOL (teaching English to speakers of other languages) book series, highlights the expectations and steps required to complete some of the final projects often linked to obtaining accredited TESOL certification. This includes the place and importance of the practicum, steps in involved in portfolio development, and the academic and scholarly rigor involved in researching and submitting a thesis. As a result, the text will help any educator if they wish to engage in further study at the graduate level. It will also help those that have colleagues or family members embarking upon a career in education to better understand many of the varied aspects of the processes involved when studying to become an educator.

Other books in the series are: *Perspectives and Practice; Implementations; Sound, Meaning, and Form;* and, *Resources.*

About the Author

David Kent is an Associate Professor at the Endicott College of International Studies, Woosong University, Republic of Korea. He provides teacher education through the TESOL-MALL Graduate Program, where he also serves as Head of Department and coordinates an academic study skills program for doctoral students.

David is also a long-standing member of the academic community with a principal research focus that revolves around the digitalization of language learning. Serving as conference plenary and keynote, as well as invited speaker, he has won a number of teacher association and conference presentation awards.

To date, he has published a number of books, including *Teaching with Technology: Integrating Technology into the TESOL Classroom*, *Internet in Education: Integrating the Internet into the TESOL Classroom*, and a *TESOL Strategy Guide* series that focuses on the use of specific digital tools for teaching. He has also authored a number of multimedia applications.

Currently, he serves on the editorial board of several journals, and his research articles have been published at the Scopus and SSCI levels in such periodicals as *Teaching English with Technology* (IATEFL), *The Journal of Asia TEFL* (Asia TEFL), and *Language Learning and Technology (NFLRC,* University of Hawai'i at Mānoa/ COERLL, University of Texas).

Issues in TESOL: Capstone Projects

2021년 6월 1일 초판 1쇄 발행

저　자	David Kent
발 행 인	존 엔디컷
발 행 처	우송대학교 출판부
주　소	대전광역시 동구 동대전로 171 우송대학교
전　화	042-630-9662
팩　스	042-630-9667
E-Mail	wsubook@wsu.ac.kr
출판등록	1998년 12월 23일 No. 1998-000013

비매품

ISBN-979-11-6110-114-9(13740)

*이 책의 저작권은 저자와 출판사에 있습니다.

*양측의 서면 동의 없이 무단 전재 및 복사를 금합니다.

www.ingramcontent.com/pod-product-compliance
Ingram Content Group UK Ltd.
Pitfield, Milton Keynes, MK11 3LW, UK
UKHW041830200726
13854UKWH00002BA/916